IN THE COMPANY OF DOGS

in the

the

COMPANY

of

DOGS

Dr. Jeannette Barnes, DVM

WordCrafts

Published by WordCrafts Press
Cody, Wyoming 82414
www.wordcrafts.net

CONTENTS

PART ONE
WONDER

Dogs unlock more human hearts than any other animal. They must have been with us since the first sunrise, and a world without them is inconceivable. Their acts of bravery are the stuff of legend.

Yet if we imagine ourselves at a primordial roaring campfire, when we knew them only as wolves circling and howling, teasing out our weaknesses, we would have been hard pressed to believe we could ever be partners.

The first part of this book relates myths and stories about dogs, showing that without the intimate connection resulting from domestication, neither we nor dogs could have progressed to where we are today. Dogs co-developed with us. We took baby steps with them until the time was ripe for us to spread over the earth.

CHAPTER ONE

DOGS IN PARADISE

The earth trembled.
A great rift appeared separating the first man from the rest of the animal kingdom.
As the chasm widened, all the other animals returned to the forests, where they lived
in paradise.
But the dog leaped the chasm.
His love for humanity was greater than his bond to other creatures.
He willingly forfeited his place in paradise to prove it.

~Ojibwa Legend,
Told by Native Americans in the Great Lakes region

Embedded in paradise as tightly as the gem in a treasured ring, the gray wolf torses her body to bite and chew at her side. Her breaths come in short gasps: "hut, hut, hut." She stumbles, initially dragging one rear leg, then the other. Finally toppling over, she forces her backbone against the packed dirt. She must free her body of the pups she carries, or they will bind her up internally, and she will die a slow, tormented death.

The wolf begins open-mouthed breathing, forcing oxygen into straining lungs and muscles. The litter is larger than she has ever carried, and is complicated by the breech presentation of the puppy with the odd-shaped head. Rippling contractions of her uterus become uncoordinated, and the impatient life within is tossed back and forth like a lifeboat in a sea at storm. The precious cargo in this wolf is of greater than usual importance because the odd-shaped puppy is an immature dog. Bearing an un-wolf-like short snout and wide palate, this puppy is waiting for her encounter with man.

"Ya-woo," bleats the mother, seeking to find a position to ease her agony. Then with a rush of fluids and a final yelp, the little creature is delivered tail end first. The mother reaches to clean the pup, and others come out in a rush. Her male companion and other members of the pack will provide her and the pups with food, as none of the other females will accept a mate this season.

She nurses them all, even the odd one, whose eyelids and ears eventually open the same way as the wolf puppies. The pup stays with her mother until she is strong enough to walk through paradise on her own power, seek her own mate and reproduce.

Then the life cycle repeats itself.

Reproduce.

Feed and protect young.

In each generation of nine to twelve months, there appear small changes to the boney structure of the face, the mandible, the teeth. Not involving every pup in the litter, but enough puppies that overall a new set of beings comes to life.

Dogs.

Something like this could happen. Something like this did happen.

Time passes.

Millennia pass.

Many generations later, the wolf turns up again. This time,

it is in a boneyard. A gigantic gravesite in Czechoslovakia with over four thousand skeletons of canids: wolves, foxes, and dogs. Where did they come from?

The history of the dog cannot be told independently of the history of man. In addition to this unprecedented finding of fossilized wolves and dogs, there are human skeletons. Some thirty thousand years ago, a tiny community of people banded together and left their mark on the earth. It is very likely that this is the first grouping of people who involved themselves with wolves and dogs.

Life is raw for this clan of seventy to one hundred human beings.

They live a heartbeat away from nature.

Their environment is shared with fantastical beasts. Woolly mammoths with twelve-foot tusks, thick pelts, and pearlescent toenails dominate the land. Only slightly shorter in stature, another creature with impressive ivory shares their territory. The woolly rhino stands six feet tall at the shoulder and can easily grow to fourteen feet in length.

More familiar beasts also populate the landscape: reindeer, rabbits and bear.

And dogs.

Though these canines are not as large as a full grown human being, they nevertheless weigh in at nearly eighty pounds. With a squashed backbone and bowed legs, it is easy to surmise that they carry heavy burdens for the tribe. Considering the number of mammoth bones lying around—the remains of well over a thousand animals—many scientists believe that dogs acted as pack animals to carry the bulk of the mammoth parts and pieces from the hunting grounds back home.

The typical dog eats well. Her wide-set jaws with unique

molar teeth can bring down a reindeer. These jaws and short snout have come under intense scrutiny in the present day because they are part of scant proof that she is not a wolf either of the present or the past. Her teeth are worn and cracked. There is a good chance she suffers daily pain due to exposed roots in her mouth, but like Fido of the twenty-first century, she must eat and will do so no matter the pain. And she lives to a ripe old age—somewhere between four and eight years.

This animal's parents and grandparents are surely dogs, but earlier than this time period, her heritage is hazy. Recent predecessors are definitely not wolves, but she can breed with a male wolf if she so desires. From the number of wolf skeletons in the graveyard, there appear to be many opportunities. What differentiates her from other canids is this: she serves man willingly.

The civilization she supports is brilliant. At a time when the contemporaries of this clan are wandering the earth, pulling up plants for nutrition and finding the occasional hare to eat, these prehistoric people are reaping the benefits of personalized hunting techniques. Furthermore, they protect themselves from winter blizzards that frequent this region, unlike the hunter-gatherers. Tribal members fashion thick-walled boney enclosures made from the skeletons of mammoths and rhinoceroses.

Toolmakers already exist at this point in time, and are in demand for finely splitting the flint rocks which will be fashioned into brutish knives or the business end of a harpoon. From the carcass, they extricate and clean towering pelvis and rib bones, anchor them in the ground, and elevate them skyward to provide a scaffolding for homes. Families dry rescued skins in the sun and wind, stretched out on a frame of bones to deter shrinkage. Stripped meat is made into lengths appropriate to be placed in the sun and dried for later meals. Everything is saved for later use.

Seamstresses are also highly valued. Bone needles are found which were apparently used to make sufficient holes in the dried skins so that, much like present day sewing, someone could pull a string of dried intestine or fine strip of meat through both layers and thereby knit the skins together. The skins could be wrapped like a second skin over the bone shelter and be tight protection against the weather.

A further function of properly dried and prepared bones is to utilize them in bonfires to ward off intruders, human or otherwise. Smaller domestic fires are used to warm the family hut so that kin can move about without their bulky clothing.

Unbelievable as it may seem, neighboring clans of this time period produce some of the oldest pottery on the planet. Lumps of clay are fashioned into animal bodies, then scoured with ground-up bone and fired. Twentieth century explorers discover reindeer, hares, rhinos, mammoths, wolves and other creatures from these leavings. Scientists find kiln remnants. Though undoubtedly the kiln fired at a low temperature, it fulfilled the remarkable purpose of sustaining the pieces from the thrashing forces of nature.

The most famous piece is the diminutive 'Black Venus' with pendulous breasts, wide hips and etched markings along her back representing her backbone. Current thinking is that she is a fertility symbol, but it's also conceivable that she oversaw the hunt.

Tribal people go after prey like hungry people do—with overabundant numbers of men to assure success. No one knows whether this tribe used dogs to hunt mammoths. It is a fact, however, that instinct drives packs of dogs to surround beasts much larger than themselves, confound the senses, and then strike from multiple angles. Fighting dogs are expert at locking their jaws around a tender part of their prey, and holding on while being thrashed about by a much larger adversary.

Locating and trapping the mammoth is the duty of the males of the tribe. To ensure success, a group of men starts out to look for fresh tracks and tufts of fur from the woolly behemoth. Once located, they propel the mammoth herd sometimes for miles into a valley with steep sides, surrounding the beasts from above. They choose a member of the herd that seems fragile, perhaps a straggler or elderly animal. All attention is focused on that one mammoth.

However, like elephants of the present, the creatures look out after their own, stomping and bellowing and forming a ring around the babies and weak members of their herd. They present a formidable row of tusks to invaders.

Aim and force are of the essence. Men must sink the harpoon deeply, penetrating the wiry wool through the unforgiving skin, and into the beating heart. One slight miscalculation, and the animal will crush them for their effort. This is why early stone spears have given way to the ivory harpoon, a hefty six-foot-long killing device possessed of greater accuracy and range than any spear.

Whatever their methods are, clan members do not have long to rejoice, as other members of the mammoth herd are close by and can turn on them at any instant. Paralyzing a man or piercing an organ is a real possibility. It is surmised that the tribe has likely gotten very clever at avoiding this tragedy by using dogs in the hunt.

One of the ironies of life for the clan is that mammoth bones and tusks are required to capture more mammoths. But nearly 100% of the clan's diet, shelter, and weapons come from this source. One of the successes this group enjoys over the hunter-gatherers is that their skill at hunting and building provides protection and food to the most vulnerable. The very young and the very old are much less at risk with a constant food source, fire rings, and houses.

Yet not everyone survives the winter.

Because of the difficulty of digging deeply in permafrost, people's bodies are buried and re-buried in mass graves covered with a protective layer of mammoth shoulder bones. Some bodies are hoisted in the air to protect them from scavenging animals. These elevated bodies fill a dedicated section of the graveyard.

A very special woman is buried nearby, separated from other graveyard inhabitants. Artifacts to assist her in the afterlife fill her grave. She is unearthed in the present day with a foxtail gripped in her fingers, and her face appears at first to have an ugly snarl. But on closer observation the severe distortion of her face and crushed eye socket become clearer. She had a disfiguring injury. Interred with her is a specially carved figurine of rhinoceros or mammoth ivory mimicking her heavily scarred face.

She is a shaman, scientists believe. A shaman is a seer that acts as intermediary between the known world and the unseen worlds, and therefore has great spiritual knowledge. She keeps at bay the unseen world, providing protection and guidance. This woman carries her foxtail to cement her authoritarian relationship with her people. The seer is an emotional and spiritual example for her clan.

Delving into the emotional and spiritual attachment between people and dogs during prehistory requires a visit to fossilized evidence. With thousands of dog and wolf bones eerily present, what conclusions can we draw? Or is there a better approach?

At one time in this ancient civilization, a person not so different from you and I decided to bury his dog. Because burying a dog is commonplace in contemporary society, it may be difficult to appreciate the grueling action required to accomplish this act. First, this group of people lived on permafrost, where the ground was literally hard as ice. Less than two dozen people have been found in a final resting place below ground. This illustrates what a feat it was to inter any creature deep enough to evade roaming predators. Second, the dog was not merely placed in an opening in the ground. Her body was prepared for the afterlife in several ways. An extraordinarily large mammoth bone was placed into her mouth, allowing her to ease into the unknown hunting grounds of the next world.

Finally, her brain was removed from her braincase, using a spear or other sharp-pointed instrument to break through the skull bones.

What can we surmise from this startling set of facts? What do we know about these people?

At the very least it is proof of a unique relationship, most likely a treasured union between a dog and a human being. It is proof that the final voyage for this dog is very carefully and purposefully arranged.

This uncannily beautiful and productive society is creative, inventive, brave, loyal, and artistic. They raise their children in such a way as to be good hunters and providers, too. At the very heart of their relationship with dogs is the question of how they viewed them. Can we discover this in a modern society, or at least draw a parallel?

Our ancient Czechoslovakian dog with the holes in his braincase is interred near three other similarly treated skulls and several wolf skulls as well. Interestingly, contemporary people that live near the north pole perform ceremonies on recently dead predatory animals that which may help clarify certain of the acts of the ancients.

Indigenous people of the circumpolar region believe the skeleton is the container or representative of the soul or the spirit. They make holes over the braincase of foxes, wolves, bears, and other predators. Some societies even separate the animals' heads from the body.

Several spiritual reasons are offered for this practice:

1) This practice allows the spirit to leave.

2) This practice fulfills a 'sending back' ceremony. The belief is that when wolves or foxes are killed, their souls are sent back to their origin in such a respectful way that the fox or wolf will speak nicely of man and encourage other game animals to approach people, thus easing the difficulty of hunting.

3) This practice appeases the dead animal's spirit, thus inviting him to come back to the material plane.

4) This practice allows the brain to be eaten as communion with the tribe of which he was a part.

Are these similarities persuasive that a type of spirituality existed in the earlier culture as well? It appears possible that dogs filled a segment of society in which they were loved and revered and met the deepest yearning needs of human beings, very similar to now.

I believe families in this culture felt Paradise, felt the

essence of their dog, and their dog felt the connection also. Dogs in this society made a practice of responding as no other creature ever had previously to human wishes and needs, to the desires of playing and protection of children.

The dog's mind was aligned to theirs, and losing this animal was akin to losing a comrade. They wept. Their family mourned. They gave her a bone that she didn't have to work for. And then they buried her, deep, safe, away from predators; for this little piece of Paradise to be unearthed twenty-seven-thousand years later with a mystery and story to be elaborated by those who love dogs.

DOGS AS GODS

PART 1
ANUBIS

Dogs are regarded as members of society in many cultures. In this case, a dog was elevated to the role of god.

I am Anubis, Absolute Ruler of the Underworld. I am Egyptian. My face and arms are black, and my ears stick upright out of the top of my head. I have thick legs that taper to a fine, upright heel, with paws that allow me to pivot in my work. Some people have referred to me as a jackal, or a wolf. Those canids could not withstand the rigors of my job.

I am an embalmer. A mummifier. In ancient times, I raided cemeteries and dug up freshly buried corpses to consume them. But no longer. I now preserve death.

In addition, I judge the dead. In fact, I am the Guardian of the Scales. No one else has such an important role as me. When a dead person is brought before me, I take my instructions directly from the Book of the Dead. I am told to follow Ma'at, or truth. Ma'at involves the propriety of the person's life, and it is symbolized by a feather. I place the feather on one side of the Scale of Judgment and the person's heart on the other.

If the feather is heavier, I ascend with the dead person to further existence in Heaven.

If the heart is heavier than the feather, then at once the person is consumed by a female demon, Ammit, who is known as "the devourer of the dead."

Thus, the dead are an example to the living. This is my role.

I also protect the tombs of the dead. Those that inhabit the tombs carve my likeness into the walls where they wish protection. They write prayers to me so that I may better fulfill my role.

How, you may ask, did I leave the role of desecrator of corpses and take on the role of protector?

Simply, the Gods asked for my help. Let me be specific. There were two brother gods, Osiris and Set. Osiris was the oldest, and he became King or Pharaoh. But Set never forgave his brother for taking the throne rather than letting Set become ruler. The younger brother therefore transformed himself into a monster, and slashed Osiris to bits. Then he scattered the parts of his body all over Egypt. It is rumored that one of the most essential parts of his anatomy was never located.

Osiris' wife was inconsolable, and she asked me and her sister to help restore her husband. We searched throughout Egypt, and recovered all his mutilated pieces except for one of the most intimate, which was never found. Exactly as he was, I wrapped him in linen. Thus, I was given the name "He who is in the place of embalming."

My goddess Isis filled Osiris with the breath of life. As is the way with a god, even though he is missing his phallus, he has a son. Even with his beloved offspring to occupy his time, he has spent many hours with me in the Underworld conducting worthy souls to Heaven. Our work is crucial.

If the person is not mummified properly, with a proper "opening of the mouth" ritual, that person will not be able to speak or eat once they are dead. Overseeing these processes is not an easy task.

After my daughter Kebechet was grown, I enlisted her help with proper embalming. As she is the goddess of purification, she could not put up with the smell of putrefaction. At times, people would try to cut corners and not use the sweetly odorous herbs and plants, so we had to take the extra step of smelling all the corpses. It is not difficult for me to see who is trying to skimp by using inferior processes.

I am a dog, a very special dog. Much like your cadaver-smelling dogs of the present, I have specialized work to perform, and perform well.

I wish I could tell you exactly who my birth parents are, but like many dogs of later generations, my parentage is shrouded in mystery. Legend has it that my mother was Nephthys, the Goddess of Darkness and my father was Osiris. But others have told me that I come from a direct lineage of Bastet, the cat-headed warrior goddess. In that case, I would have the privilege of being sired by Ra, the sun god himself. That is the version that I favor. If I had not been chosen as the embalming god, I would have liked to be a warrior.

It is not difficult to see why a cult has grown up around me. People throughout Egypt worship me. I defeated nine of Egypt's enemies, and was thus given a special seal so that I could place it on the tomb once it has been filled with its occupant. Because of my overwhelming knowledge of anatomy, I have been referred to as the overseer of anesthesiology. My knowledge of healing plants inspires many.

I have been given the responsibility over innumerable

priests that carry out my work to the letter. Only they are allowed to wear my mask when carrying out the process of embalming.

My cult center is in Cynopolis. This word translated means "city of the dog." Cults required you to perform a series of rituals that purified you and made you worthy. These ceremonies also give homage to your particular god. It is necessary to worship a god through a cult so that favor will come to you.

If you are so honored, you may keep a shrine in your quarters by housing dogs and puppies. Not just everyone is allowed to be so honored. Many can only worship with groups of other devotees.

Though I have been overseer of the dead for these three thousand years, I am aware of what happens throughout Egypt to the living, especially animals. In Memphis, a black bull with a white triangle and crescent moon on his chest and white spots on his flanks has become an oracle. His name is Apis. He lives at a temple there. During the day, he is led into a stable where he is allowed to make one of two choices: to the right or to the left.

People needing divine inspiration come to get answers from Apis. They can ask a yes or no question and see if the bull goes to the right or left for their answer. I may personally believe that they could get their answer much more quickly from a dog than a bull, but that is not my role. I am justly proud that animals are consulted on important matters.

As time goes by, more and more people make pilgrimages to Memphis and other cult centers. They want to prove their loyalty to sacred animals. Many priests have become employed tending millions of ibis birds and crocodiles as well as puppies and dogs so that people are able to properly bless their gods through monetary offerings and ritual animal blessings.

For this reason, the gods have extended their existence through these thousands and even millions of animals. Pilgrims want to take them home or have them ritually buried. The only practical way is through mummies.

I take credit not only for human embalming, but for starting the practice of dog burials and mummifications. It is a sacred duty. Under my direction certain priests are given permission to wear my mask when they mummify animals. This ensures quality. I personally know of eight million mummified dogs residing in the catacombs at Saqqara that have been prepared for sincere patrons.

King Tut knew of my skills. He prepared a statue of me lying in my prone and ready position, anxious to serve my king. The sleigh I rest on was a perfect presentation for me to be carried in the funeral procession at his untimely death. He placed me looking at the setting sun to guide him as he moved into the afterlife. Of course, I oversaw his embalming and directed it with great care.

In my spare time, I observe other dogs. They are referred to as iwiw, which is supposed to reflect the noise they make when they bark. I personally could have chosen a better word, but iwiw is sort of charming. Many dogs among the living are adored by family members. They wear collars with their names inscribed. My favorite is the name 'Useless,' but I see many that are more reflective of helping roles such as 'Good Herdsman,' 'Brave One,' and 'Reliable.'

Egyptians use their dogs for protection and hunting. They are even used as enforcers for the police. I have seen their depictions many times in tombs, and their important role in

Egyptian life pleases me greatly. It is an extension of my life's work to see them treated with care during the thousands of years I have reigned.

Sadly for me, the bulk of my work will now be overseen by Osiris, another god. After he was restored to life, his interests changed, and he will phase me out of the work I love. But the contributions I have made will be treasured for many centuries longer than I have already served.

Everyone will remember the dog who served Egypt.

DOGS AS GODS

PART 2
SAMARA

This Hindu goddess-dog saved daylight and in so doing, mankind.

My name is SaramA.

I am a dog-god, and I sit at the right hand of Indra, Hindu king of all gods.

To know more about our relationship, you first must know more about Indra. This king of all gods is not born in the usual way, but is so special and pure that he comes out of the mouth of the Primordial God. This god of all gods is named Perusha. He takes special time and care fashioning Indra, making certain that when his progeny takes the throne, he has the ability to rule lightning, thunder, storms, and rivers.

Besides the gifts of ruling nature, Indra is also a great warrior.

Sadly, that is the easiest part of my story to tell. What I wish to relate comes from the Hindu sacred text called the Mahabharata, which is rich and colorful but very confusing at times. Tales about me have been rewritten so many times so that I cannot always remember my own history. I will be as clear as I can.

For the gods, day turning to night and night turning to day is an eternal struggle between two forces. The day-force is called Devas. It is all about light. The night-force does not have a name because it is stolen, and we do not want to deify it by calling it a name. In any case, that force is only about the absence of light. We know that the sun's rays are stolen by the night and that every morning, dawn must rescue light from the darkness.

In our religion, the hoarding of the sun's light by the darkness eventually became associated with merchants. The reason is that merchants were believed to hoard goods and money. These hoarders of the sun's light (and possibly money and goods) are portrayed as envious demons named PaNis.

Every day, Indra wants to recover the rays of light. Here's where it gets complicated. Somehow, these rays of light become referred to as cows. Maybe the writer of the Mahabharata believed that as a dog, I would be more adept at finding these cows than rays of light. So, I was put on the scent of finding stolen cows.

When I arrived at the hidden cave of the cows, in a place far beyond the mythical river RasA, the PaNis mocked me and my god. The PaNis said that the cows were theirs and that Indra was just jealous of the demons' possessions. If they were just cows, it wouldn't matter so much. But if they were rays of light, it was essential for me to get them back.

So, the PaNis tried to bribe me. They told me I could have leadership over some of the cows, and that I could align myself with them and be wealthy. Of course, because of my allegiance to the brave Indra, I did not fall for this trick. (Though some verses in the Mahabharata imply that I was very tempted, or even did align with the PaNis. I would die a thousand deaths first!) The rays of light are necessary for all of us to stay out of darkness. Even the PaNis need the light, though they may not be aware of it.

What happened next is unfortunate. There was a battle. As I said, my Indra is a brave warrior who also controls thunder and lightning. The PaNis did not have a chance to win. They were soundly defeated.

I am lucky and grateful that my god gave me additional names as the result of my faithfulness. I am now Devu-suni, the female dog of the gods. I later gave birth to two sons, whom I named Shyama and Sabala. Unlike me, they each have four eyes and are brindle-colored. Also unlike me, they are messengers of Yama, who is the original Lord of the Law. Later, Yama became the God of Death. This opened channels for my boys to step in for service.

I am proud to say that my boys guard the path to heaven. They protect men and women on their path to heaven.

My stature has been further elevated. Not only am I the mother of all dogs, but the mother of all beasts of prey, including lions and tigers.

I am all at once a beast, a spirit, the right hand of a god, the mother of those who protect men, and the vital spirit that brings forth predatory animals.

All things to all men. The more functions I can serve, the more I wish to serve.

CHAPTER THREE

DOGS AS FOSSILS

Nagaicho, the creator, set out to create the world, and he took along the dog. He placed big pillars at the corners of the earth to hold up the sky. He created man from dirt, then woman.

The sun became hot. The moon was cold, and trees grew everywhere. Waves danced on the surface of the ocean, and all the creatures of the seas swam and were happy. Nagaicho saw that creatures of the earth needed water. He dragged his feet deep into the earth and created rivers. He poked his fingers into the earth and formed springs. Elk and deer came to drink.

"Drink," Nagaicho said to the dog. And the dog drank from the sweet water. Nagaicho lay down and drank.

"It is good. They will all drink it," said Nagaicho.

Nagaicho piled rocks around the water to make lakes and ponds.

"Drink, my dog," and the dog drank. Nagaicho plunged his face into the water and drank.

"It is good. Bears and people will drink here."

Nagaicho put salamanders and fish and turtles in the creeks. He put grizzlies and deer in the forests and panthers and jack rabbits.

Nagaicho walked along creating creatures. He made the trees tall. He made acorns and chestnuts. He put berries in the bushes and birds and snakes. He made grasshoppers.

"We made it, my dog. We are nearly home now. I will drink water. You too drink."

The face of the earth was covered with growing things. Creatures were multiplying on it. Nagaicho went back into the north with his dog.

~From the Kato,
a group of California Native Americans

"Where did I come from?"

Though I am interested in the answer to this question, I am much more intrigued by the answer to "Where do puppies come from?" or even "Why do dogs and people figure so intimately in each other's history?"

In this book, you will read differing versions of the origin of the dog. You will see that when these stories are birthed, the origins of the dog and the origins of civilization are often intertwined. Though the particularly lovely myth of Nagai-cho provides the contentment which comes from simplicity and order, some stories told about dog's origins are bizarre. This may be because the origin of the dog is hotly contested by those in the know. The location, timing, and purpose for which the dog came into being is extremely controversial.

Zooarcheologists, those scientists who study animal fossils, argue about whether dogs originated in China, in an area south of the Yangtze River, or in Europe. We know they accompanied early man over the Bering Strait into North America. But where was their birthplace? Could there possibly be multiple areas of domestication?

Part of the issue is how to interpret the fossilized remains of a living being. People argue about such questions as: when was there an animal that was absolutely a dog, and absolutely not a wolf? Were they domesticated purposefully? Can we actually tell the age and species of this fossil?

Scientists agree on one principle: because dogs continued to cross-mate with wolves throughout their history, it is nearly impossible to find a well-defined "first dog."

Tantalizing specimens of creatures such as a dog-like wolf or wolf-like dog have been discovered in a cave in

Belgium dating from approximately sixteen thousand years ago. Another discovery is from a very early Israeli site where a four-month-old puppy is found buried with an elderly man. These are very patchy beginnings on which to hang one's hat about the origin of this species. And they do not answer the questions of what caused animals to breach the gap of wildness and become a close companion of man. Besides the Czechoslovakian and Israeli sites, there are very few ancient examples of the closeness of man and beast living together. This does not, however, dissuade researchers from speculating why wolves metamorphosed and became part of the human family.

Some claim that it must have been wolves taking the first steps. Their logic runs something like this, "They probably saw the leavings of a hunt and went after the scraps. The little ones were likely less aggressive, and were able to make friends with the people rather than try to be like the larger, predatory wolves."

Others are not so sure.

Dr. Pang, a geneticist and careful researcher, banded together with a group of like-minded scientists to attempt to find answers to precisely these questions. They relied on specialized DNA that is a part of every cell in every wolf and dog.

The genetic material is passed basically intact from one generation to the next through the mother's egg alone. None of this information is passed through the sperm cell; thus, it allows offspring to be assessed using only the mother's information. This allows the scientists to trace a pure line of heredity back through countless generations.

After intense study on the maternal heredity of dogs, Pang's team arrived at stunning conclusions.

The full range of (canine) genetic diversity was found only in southeastern Asia south of the Yangtze River. The main mtDNA sequence...indicates an origin 5400 to 16,300 years ago from at least 51 female wolf founders.

Their research honed in on one birthplace of the dog, south of the Yangtze River. Further stunning conclusions followed.

These results indicate that the domestic dog originated in southern China less than 16,300 years ago, from several hundred wolves. The place and time coincide approximately with the origin of rice agriculture, suggesting that the dogs may have originated among sedentary hunter-gatherers or early farmers, and the numerous founders indicate that wolf taming was an important culture trait.

The researchers imply several thought-provoking points. First, that for some reason, people along the Yangtze River felt an overwhelming need to domesticate wolves; that is to bring these snarling, hostile, dangerous animals into their camps and villages. Not only that, but Pang implies that these wolf-taming experts held culturally significant roles in the society of their time.

Second, they draw the conclusion that this domestication process of wolves occurred at approximately the same time as domestication of people, when they began to abandon a roaming way of life for that of farming. Did they need each other to become domesticated?

When wolves were tamed, what was their function? Companions? Co-hunters? Workers? Burden bearers? Trash scavengers? Entertainment? Nutrition? Surely early people did not have an excess of time to whittle away with trivial pursuits, so what need did the wolves fulfill?

Thousands of miles distant from China, Olaf Thalmann

and his team of researchers have put their own set of eyes on dog fossils and dog genetics.

Eons before Pang's dogs elicited the slightest twinkle in their mothers' eyes, according to Thalmann, European canines walked the earth. They left skulls and other bones as evidence; evidence that can be dated with a fairly good degree of accuracy.

Was this the original event when a wolf give birth to a dog?

Dr. Thalmann takes a further step. Not content to be merely at the head of the pack, he elucidates the complete canine mitochondrial DNA code in 2013. He knows who is a dog and who isn't.

Thalmann's theorizes that all modern dogs derive from European wolves. That initial cataclysmic event, where wolves began giving birth to dogs, occurred sometime in the wide sweep of time between 18,800 and 32,100 years ago.

What would science be without controversy? Other scientists have stepped in with other theories. Critics state that dogs from China have been left out of Thalmann's work. This is true. And conversely, Pang did not include European dogs in his study. However, the European dogs barked, chewed bones, and played fetch five thousand years earlier than even the oldest Chinese dogs.

It seems apparent with the knowledge that we have so far that more than 30,000 years ago, a sort of wolf-like creature was drawn to men at the same time that men needed dogs. They started interacting, perhaps because flashes of inspiration lead man to approach wolf pups or certain wolves took to humans. Relatively few canine generations passed as the incipient dogs became easier to handle, to train. Their bodies and their brains changed as they were domesticated.

The constant presence of humans affected both species, as they co-developed.

I think it is thrilling that there appear to be multiple domestication events across the globe, at different times. If the need for co-domestication of dog and man existed, then carrying it out in several places was only a matter of time.

Maybe the time was ripe for numerous dances with wolves.

DOGS AS HUMAN BEINGS

PART 1
GIRL WITH RED PAINT

Some myths show the relationship between dogs and people as being so firmly entwined that they involve the actual melding of the two. What follows are two such myths from completely different cultures. One is from Native American lore, and the other is from Ireland, a Celtic myth of a talented archer and huntsman.

Once there was a girl who lived near the mouth of the Fraser River. She refused all offers of marriage.

At last a strange young man visited her at night and lay with her. She wondered who he could be, and made up her mind to mark him. She put red paint on the palms of her hands; and when he appeared the following night in the dark, she embraced him, leaving the imprints of her hands on his sides.

It was her habit to never go out of the house, but the next morning she went out to see if she could recognize the young man. All the young men were playing, and called out, "Oh, see the girl! She has come to see us play."

As none of them had any marks, she went home. When near the house, she saw her father's large dog being fed by her mother, and on his sides were her hand-marks.

Her mother said, "Who has been making a fool of the dog by painting his sides?"

The girl was ashamed, went in, and cried to herself. In due time she gave birth to eleven pups—five male and six female. One of the latter was half black and half white. The people were very angry. They beat the dog nearly to death, and left the girl and her children to die.

When they were gone, the dog became a man, and went into the woods, where he healed himself. The pups were hungry: therefore, their mother went at night with a torch to dig clams on the beach during ebb-tide.

On her return, when near the house, she heard the pups dancing, and singing, "She thinks we are dogs, but we are children."

The black and white one was on watch, and warned the others of their mother's approach; so, they all hastily donned their skins and kept quiet. She looked about, and saw children's tracks where they had been dancing.

She said, "It is strange that you are dogs, and still you give no warning, nor tell when strangers are around dancing."

The following night, when she went out after clams, she decided to fool her children with a deception. She took her robe off at the beach, placed it on a stick, tied her torch to another stick by its side, and hurried home.

The pups saw the robe and torch at the beach and thought she was still there, and kept on dancing and singing. She crept up stealthily, so she could surprise the black and white one who was on watch. She then seized the skins of the others before they could get them, and threw them into the fire. Thus, they remained children, while the black and white one remained a dog.

Their father returned in the form of a good looking man, and hunted for the family. He killed many goats and deer, and soon had great quantities of meat and fat. He put much fat into the caches of those people who had left some fish for his hungry girlfriend, and into the caches of those who had left nothing he put only bones.

The girl's grandmother pitied her, and sent Crow with some fish for her. Because of this, Dog-Man gave Crow fat to take back to the old woman, and by this it became known how wealthy the girl had become.

Then the people all welcomed her again, and were fed by Dog-Man.

~The Dog Children
A legend from Native American Uta'mqt people

CHAPTER FOUR
DOGS AS HUMAN BEINGS

PART 2
BRAN

Let me introduce myself. I am Bran, Irish Wolfhound extraordinaire. Or Wolfhound byordinar, as I prefer to call myself in my native Gaelic. I am a mythical creature, but that should not spoil your enjoyment. I am so massive that a normal sized Wolfhound could run under my body without touching my underside. My shoulders reach a full-grown man's chest.

Am I boasting? I don't mean to. I go into depth about my canine features merely because under the right circumstances, I would have been born a man. I feel that I should be completely honest about the reasons why this did not occur.

I belong to a man, or rather the Lord of the Hunt, Fionn mac Cumhaill. He is a Robin Hood-type of fellow, a wandering woodland character with a band of men who support him. He is actually my cousin by blood. How this came about involves one of those human emotions that is difficult for a dog to understand: jealousy. Especially when it involves breeding.

People should either decide that it is fine to have sex with everyone, and never be jealous, or always be faithful to one another. But they cannot decide, and thus there is jealousy. I am only jealous when some dog gets a bigger bone than I do.

But I digress, which I often do, because there is so much to tell. My aunt Tuirrean fell in love with a man named Iollan. She didn't confide in me whether she was aware that in his youth, her husband was lovers with Uchtdealb (a faery queen and one of the magical people who ruled Ireland before the coming of the Celts). But it wouldn't have mattered if she had all the facts. Uchtdealb thirsted for revenge, and dreamt up a plan to make Iollan fall out of love with my aunt. The faery queen disguised herself as a messenger. Under false pretenses, she led my aunt into the woods and promptly took out a hazel wand, transforming my aunt into an Irish Wolfhound. Things were a bit complicated by the fact that my aunt was already pregnant with Iollan's twins.

One of those twins was me.

Of course, if it was necessary to be transformed into a dog, the best of all possible worlds would be the noblest of breeds, the Irish Wolfhound. Still, those days in the womb during my metamorphosis were quite rocky.

But to continue the events leading up to my birth. Uchtdealb brought my aunt (in dog form) to one of Fionn's friends, telling him that she was a gift from Fionn. Fionn's friend Fergus hated dogs and did not want to keep her, but the faery queen was very conniving and proposed that my aunt would be a fabulous hunter. Uchtdealb then threw in the ultimate tidbit about my aunt being pregnant, and that she must not be overworked near the time of the birth. Not at all convinced, Fergus nevertheless adopted my aunt and called her by her human name, Tuirrean. While using my aunt's talents in the field, Fergus found out that she was indeed a hunter byordinar and he was won over by her personality.

When the end of my aunt's pregnancy drew near, Fergus rested her from hunting and she gave birth to beautiful Wolfhound puppies, my sister and me. We were given to Fionn. Because of all the gossip about the whole thing, Fionn knew we were cousins, and the three of us were bound together with unbreakable thread. When we were wee puppies, we just adored him, but when we grew, we were his hunters and protectors. We grew into our Wolfhound nature more as dogs than humans, and it reflected in our bodies.

To give you an idea of how others saw us as adults, read the description that follows. Legend says I was black in color, and "ferocious, white breasted, sleek-haunched, with fiery deep black eyes that swim in sockets of blood." My sister Sceolan was described as "small-headed, with the eyes of a dragon, claws of a wolf, vigor of a lion, and the venom of a serpent."

With this kind of build-up, we had to be hunters. We set out early every morning with Fionn to find enough game to fill the bellies of all the Fiana tribe. Until one fateful morning, we never missed our mark. On that day we saw the most unusual red-colored deer and we pursued her with our pack. However, as we finally cornered her, something did not appear right. We scared all the other dogs off. Her human nature called to us, and we discerned that she had endured sorcery just like we had.

The deer turned out to be a woman named Sadbh. We found this out after she regained her human body upon crossing the line marking Fionn's property. She hugged us and told us that she had been the victim of Fear Doirich, a creature who made unwelcome advances. On one occasion, she mentioned that he was from the Otherworld, and on another, she just called him a druid. Little matter who he actually was, because when she rejected him, he turned her into the red deer which we pursued. He apparently had hopes that she would perish at the hands of a hunter and call it justice for her refusal.

The Wicked One's plot was foiled, because when Fionn first set eyes on Sadbh, he became entranced with the maiden, and he married her to keep her safe in his compound. But as is the way with humans, she became pregnant and like my aunt, was transformed back into another creature as soon as she left the compound.

Though Fionn was brilliant and gifted, especially after he ate the Salmon of Wisdom and gained the ability of clair-voyance and inspiration, he may have been slightly lacking in his abilities with women. He didn't know that you can't keep a woman on your property for safekeeping. She is going to want to leave, even for a few hours. There may have been a better way to protect her, but in the end, it was her decision to leave during his absence defending Ireland from invaders.

No one knows for certain, but legend says that when she left, she was turned back into a deer by her stalker. For seven years, Fionn looked for his wife using his best hunting team, Scolean and me. Fionn knew she was pregnant when she left him, and he was frantic to find the child. As fortune would have it, Fionn found a young red deer separated from its mother. The humanness in my sister and me recognized sorcery again, and we brought the young deer into our fold where he changed to a young boy, mute, scared, and shivering from exposure. Fionn wrapped him in his cloak and brought him back to the fortress, where he eventually learned to talk and spoke lovingly of the deer mother who took care of him all his life. My cousin named him Oisin which means "little deer." I am told that he writes excellent poems and mythology, but being unable to read, I must take the word of others on this point.

Fionn obviously loved the child, as he spent less and less time with us. Scolean and I had to make do with playing with toys and slobbering on pieces of rope for amusement. But eventually, Fionn decided to take up hunting for his love, and we spent seven years looking for her with not even a scent. Now you understand when I say there came a time when I failed in the hunt. Irish Wolfhounds do not want to admit defeat.

By the seventh year of hunting, Scolean and I were ancient Wolfhounds and though our noses and desires were willing, our bodies could not hold up. We heard several of his men tell Fionn to leave us behind or suffer the consequences. He could not bear to think that his wife was still out there without him, and he still thought of us as his best hunters, decrepit as we were.

In very bad weather, we started what was to be a one-day hunt. But Fionn gave the signal to cast about all morning and afternoon on that day, then a second day, and finally a third day. Sceolan, accustomed to driving herself to the point of exhaustion, nevertheless was unable to fulfill the command for the first time in her very long life. She sank to a sitting position and remained there.

Even though I, too, was spent, I nudged her and encouraged her without success. With that failure, I dragged my body and spirit from her to begin what was to be my final hunt. Fionn waited behind for long enough to signal Sceolan to wait in her sitting position, and then followed me. For some reason, I led him into craggy hills of Ceentlea.

There I caught a scent I had not smelled for over seven years. My age melted away. I began to bay and run as though I was a young hound. I could see silhouetted against the sun, beyond a small lake, a red deer standing on the edge of a cliff. I heard Fionn call out Sadbh's name. The deer turned and looked once at him, then whirled and jumped off the cliff. I looked at my master, and then followed Sadbh into the water.

Fionn's men came after him when three days more had passed. They found Scolean nearly dead in her sitting position by the lake. She had to be carried to where her master stood, knee deep in the lake, not looking to right or left, but staring where the deer and his other Wolfhound had last been seen. Scolean took her last bit of energy to wade to her master and lick his clothes, as she couldn't reach his face. Then she began a long, mournful howl that only Fionn could beseech her to quit. He gathered her broken, tired body into his arms and carried her all the way home.

When she died, he erected a cairn over her body, next to mine.

CHAPTER FIVE

DOGS AS MUMMIES

Could early Americans have survived to migrate to and populate a most unwelcoming environment without their canine companions?

After struggling for miles along the Arizona desert, car overheating and numerous stops along the way, a lucky traveler may reach Canon de Chelly. The grandeur of it all creeps up on you. First you see tantalizing bits of greenery and a thin stream meant to be a river, but nothing prepares you for the immense dimensions of the reddish, tannish rock walls with its hidden treasure.

The traveler has a sensation of being transported through the most desolate imaginable landscape, devoid of life. Yet soon after hunter-gatherers crossed the Bering Strait and introduced themselves to North America, Native Americans settled in this inhospitable area. Sure-footed and clever, they erected buildings and homes. In addition, they took advantage of the cave structure that already existed.

Searching these caves for evidence of early man takes intrepid explorers. In 1916, the Peabody Museum of Harvard University sent an expedition to determine who lived in the canyon and how they lived. Archaeologists Samuel Guernsey and Alfred V. Kidder took the challenge.

The interior of the caves is cool—about seventy degrees—but reaching them on non-existent roads in the scorching heat places a burden on the men. Water and supplies must be packed in. Insects and fatigue and occasionally mutiny must be dealt with. However, the archaeologists are fascinated.

Most of the caves yield next to nothing.

But eventually, a startling discovery is made. The notes from the approach to the cave are included here:

It might easily have escaped notice altogether, for a rider passing along the valley below would not be tempted to explore the narrow ravine leading up to it, particularly as the cliff in which it is located is apparently in full view and seems to be entirely unbroken. One short section of the cliff is, however, out of sight from the flat land, and just there is tucked away the cave.

The approach is up a tortuous ravine. Arriving below it the visitor is astonished that so great a cavern should be so effectively hidden. It occupies a commanding position in the rounded front of a buttress-like swell of the cliff. The huge portal, 120 feet across the base and at least 125 feet high, seems carved by nature to conform to the dome-shaped top of the cliff above it.

Reaching the cave after a stiff climb of 100 feet up a steep talus, one enters a spacious chamber measuring approximately 70 feet from back wall to line of shelter and 120 feet across the opening. The ceiling is high and arched, the floor rises at an easy grade from front to back. Somewhat more than half the floor space is covered by large rocks fallen from the roof, one of which measures 20 feet in length, 12 feet in width and 10 feet thick.

Within the chamber are burial areas, one with an exquisitely preserved family grouping including two well-conserved dogs.

In a large basket, an adult male Native American and an infant are curled tightly next to a large mummified dog. This dog is white or tan in color. He was about two years old when he died, and is the size of a small collie with erect ears and a long bushy tail. Thus, the name for the find: White Dog Cave.

Next to this grouping, a woman similarly buried in a basket is curled around a much smaller mummified dog, one that appears to be approximately eight months old, the size of a Terrier with short fur, erect ears and a long fully haired tail.

Many people appear to have the mistaken notion that dogs have been selectively bred for merely the past two hundred years. Here is thrilling proof that canines existed in at least two sizes, conformations, and colors thousands of years ago. The archaeologists drew the conclusion that even before this period, people had already begun selective breeding of dogs.

Photographs of these dogs, even in black and white, show the striking dissimilarities in their coat color and stature. And other than the four-footed stance and fur on their bodies, neither one resembles a wolf.

If dogs did accompany the first humans into the western Hemisphere, already diversified as to size and use, what else can we glean of their significance to earlier peoples?

Doty Fugate, past assistant curator of the Museum of Indian Arts and Culture in Santa Fe has studied over seven hundred dog burials in the area, compiling fascinating answers to just this question.

"Why study burials?" I ask her.

"Because they tell us pieces of the story, what happened when the early peoples were alive." She explains that early people had options about whether to bury their dogs, so when and how they did bury the animal is important in determining the feelings or intention of the owner. And in certain circumstances, the manner and location in which the dog was buried could have significance to the whole community.

"I'm suggesting that the dogs of the New World in the Southwest were used as a religious or spiritual escort into the next world, and sometimes they were used in certain rituals in place of people," Fugate continued.

In the past, dogs were buried at places of importance: beneath the doorway of a house, at the entrance to a city, or in other places where they could guard the structure they were buried beneath. If a place of religious significance was abandoned, a dog was often sacrificed to protect the structure.

Dogs were regularly buried with humans; sometimes with jewelry; other times with edible goods to speed their journey into the afterlife.

It is the rituals that interest me; the ways in which dogs are valued. These ancient dogs not only speak loudly for themselves, but they speak volumes about prehistoric North Americans.

"Dogs are buried alongside adults and children," Fugate says, "carefully stacked in groups, or close to important structures. They also were featured prominently in myths."

"For example, the Hopi," she said, "believe that dogs have their own kivas (underground ceremonial spiritual centers) where they retire during certain periods of the year, take off their dog identities and become human. Then they can freely discuss what is best for the tribe.

"No Hopi are supposed to hunt during this time of the year or a white tail deer will find and defeat them for their disrespect of the dog."

Fugate has unearthed an incredible variety of dogs, and believes that Native American's love and respect for dogs led them to breed for certain characteristics and functions in the household. Dogs were so integrated in the variety of household and hunting tasks that they were domesticated and selected then as they are now. She has personally found big dogs and little dogs, dogs with all colors of fur including black, tan, white, and multicolored, and dogs with different types of haircoat. She has seen curly tailed dogs, and straight tailed dogs. All this gives her assurance that selective breeding was an integral part of the prehistoric lifestyle.

Early ethnographers record almost nothing regarding the presence of dogs or about their relative sizes, even though there are photographs from the late 1800s showing multiple dogs in adobe buildings, on top of buildings, and involved in every phase of work with their masters. These scientists, present since the 1850s, are accurate in nearly every phase of the villagers' lives. Because the animals are such a fact of life and not used as a foodstuff, perhaps they are not considered worthy of note.

Fugate concludes, "Not thinking that dogs might have had a religious relationship with people means that you're leaving out a chunk of ancient religion. If you make that assumption, you are losing enormous amounts of information about the ritual context and the mindset of these people."

The religious aspects of these burial practices were

overshadowed once the Europeans came to the New World and brought their religion. Since that time, Native Americans do not follow the practices of their forebears and dogs are no longer buried.

DOGS ESCAPING DOMESTICATION

PART 1
THE NEW GUINEA SINGING DOG

For the purposes of this book, I searched for a group of dogs that has never been exposed to human beings. I wish such a dog existed; it does not. However, we can experience fascinating varieties of dogs that were once domesticated and now have returned to a wild state.

Pardon my tale if it seems choppy. My name is Kere, and I currently make my habitation at the San Diego Zoological Gardens. I am often distracted here by the sounds of other wild animals, so I cannot always concentrate on my storytelling.

I never thought that I would end up here. In the 1950s, someone classified my kin as wild animals, and so I have been brought to a place of refuge and protection from those who don't understand my rarity.

I am on display for my howl, more than anything. People seem to love it when all of us NGSD break into song, enchanting those nearby with our melody. I don't sing, but I produce a several-octave howl that when people witness it, they comment that it sends chills up their spines.

Am I a domesticated animal? Not at all, and I never have

been in the traditional sense, though I have no fear of man. No one knows, and certainly not me, how my kin became part of the planet-wide expansion of people and dogs. It is my humble belief that neither dogs nor men would be as far advanced as they are without the other, and that they would not have wandered as they did, each providing something that the other needed. But back to my story.

Some humans believe that my most likely ancient ancestor is the clever, fierce tribal dog of India and Bangladesh. (Aren't we all clever and fierce when we need to be?) The Pariah dog is referred to as a "landrace" or aboriginal dog of Asia. Some zooarcheologists believe that this aboriginal animal is the same one found in the ruins of Pompeii. That makes me part of a grand tradition whereby tribal peoples migrated and brought my grand-dogs over most of southeast Asia and Australia.

Whatever did happen, I know my ancestors were trekking through Asia ten thousand years ago, probably in an expansive mood. Someone in their party came up with the brilliant idea to take to the sea, and my kin were loaded on the boat as surely and integrally as Noah taking creatures on his ark. We were indispensable.

As we explored the sea and gigantic exotic islands, it was up to my ancestors to keep the sailors protected from the wild animals that were heard howling, chuckling, and screeching by night and by day. Eventually we set foot on land for good, at my home base in New Guinea. Over the years, my ancestors separated from humans, gravitating to the highlands. Some of us lived close to six thousand feet.

We were forgotten by human beings.

Millennia passed before outsiders noticed that we were

inhabiting the forests of New Guinea. Waves of other dogs had come to the island, and these larger mongrels suited the native peoples better than we did. We were virtually hidden from the world for a very long stretch of time. Unfortunately, in the eighteen-nineties a naturalist named Sir William Mac-Gregor procured one of my relatives. I say 'unfortunately' because it was customary at that time if one discovered a new species, the animal was sacrificed and brought to the so-called civilized world to be studied. Just as an aside, this is what happened with the duckbilled platypus, an amazing creature that was covered in fur and also had a long, curved beak like a duck. The rarest creatures were sacrificed for study. The naturalist spoke of the beautiful singing voice he had heard, but regrettably ended the life of my ancestor, rather than preserving her intact.

Nearly one hundred years passed in New Guinea before another naturalist, this time without "Sir" in front of his name, stepped on our soil. This man wished to choose life for my family members, and he returned to civilization with what he hoped would be a breeding pair of NGSD. They were brought to a native animal park run by a man named Walter Hallstrom. Hallstrom, after hearing our song, was certain that my great aunt and uncle were unlike the typical mongrel dogs of New Guinea. He packed them off to a zoo in Sydney, Australia. A specialist there returned the favor by naming our relatives after Hallstrom, declaring us to be not only wild, but a separate species named Canis hallstromi. We didn't care what they named us, only that we were allowed to live in peace.

But I have gone on too long about my history without describing what an exceptional animal comes from the likes of New Guinea. I am specially built, more like a cat than a dog in some ways, which is the other reason that humans seem so captivated by me. Though I can run at great speed when necessary, I prefer to climb trees. My forearms cup the curve of branches as I scale high points on the trees of my native land. When on the ground, my paws are soft and well-cushioned to withstand the rigors of treading rocks and boulders as I run. Like a cat, I often rub the scent of my face on the ground.

My spine is not rigidly fixed like many other species, but is flexible. I can slither in and out of tight spaces. The zoo-keeper must be cautious not to leave the smallest opening in the feeding area, or I will manipulate my spine and get out. And I am lean and small, only twenty-two pounds so that I can maneuver quickly after small prey. My eyes are beautiful and well-proportioned, with eyelids that turn up at the edges and ears that jut forward, giving me a foxlike look.

My sexual habits are quite unusual, and my behavior often attracts many suitors because of the apparent pleasure that I am experiencing. Males do not have to fight over me—I am the one who gets to be choosy. It is my unique three-minute-long howl that arouses attention. People who have heard me term it "the copulatory scream." My belly muscles contract mightily during this mating tie, indicative of the moments I spend in ecstasy. I have been gifted by Mother Nature.

I do not always get pregnant during this first encounter. The forces that rule my body will then begin another heat cycle within a few weeks, and a third cycle if necessary. It is the rule of the universe that I must carry on my species. Yet this was difficult for my family in the wild. Much like the snow leopard which also prefers high altitude, I do not travel with a pack of dogs. In the wild, humans find my solitary existence difficult to trace, just as it is burdensome for me to find a mate during breeding time.

Only a handful of us have been spotted in the wild in recent years, which is the reason I ended up in the San Diego Zoo. Everyone who thinks about us at all worries that we are extinct outside of the zoological park system. I never kept track of the numbers in my population pool, but there must have been quite a bit of inbreeding. Yet surprisingly, my friends and family have very few of the health concerns such as hip dysplasia which plague dogs that have been selectively bred. I am overjoyed to be a product of natural selection.

I am proud to be a perfectly evolved small predator.

I am absolutely not aggressive toward people. If anything, I am shy on first meeting. But I feel like I recognize humans on some very deep level. A primal level, I suppose. As in my genetic code.

I greet other dogs by submitting to them. This always seems like the smart way to go about introductions. Maybe this is why some humans think I would make a great family pet, forgetting that I am a wild animal with all the difficulties that entails. And though Hallstrom recognized my worth in the whole scheme of irreplaceable, ancient dogs, it has been only recently that other people seemed to value me as a sort of missing link.

Meanwhile, I will enjoy my life here at the zoo, singing with my contemporaries, with no other thoughts in the world.

CHAPTER SIX

DOGS ESCAPING DOMESTICATION

PART 2
FERAL DOGS IN MOSCOW

Several large cities have dog overpopulation problems to the extent that the dogs are moving away from domestication and have found their own methods to survive. Infrequently, tragedy occurs.

Several years ago, a 22-year old fashion model was making her way through the subway tunnels in Moscow. She was impeccably dressed in a black velvet hat, a blue fur-trimmed coat, short skirt and tall black boots. Her personal dog, a Staffordshire Bull Terrier, led the way. Every witness to the event agrees on these facts. Some eye-witnesses say that the feral dog living in the Mendeleyevkaya subway station, a dog named Malchik, barked at her. Another said that Malchik was sleeping near the tobacco shop where he often looked for handouts during the day. The model says that Malchik lunged at her and bit her.

No matter what led up to the horrific incident that followed, it is fact that the woman took a butcher knife out of her purse and stabbed him numerous times until he was dead. An enormous outcry occurred because of this event, and the model was forced into psychiatric treatment. The indignant people of Moscow pooled their resources to erect a statue of Malchik in the subway station. One of the women who helped install the statue said, "The question of respect to the world of animals...is the first stage of morality which one cannot skip in order to proceed to all further steps."

The issues surrounding stray dogs have been plaguing Moscow for at least one hundred fifty years. At the present time, feral animals in this city are estimated at thirty-five thousand dogs. They inhabit construction sites, streets, and as we have seen subway stations of Moscow. With a ratio of one canine per three hundred human Muscovites the animals are omnipresent.

These dogs are not small, cuddly animals, but full-size sixty or seventy-pound canines with dense straight fur, roundish ears, and black and tan or brown coats. They do not appear to be an offshoot of a specific breed, but rather formed from years of inbreeding within the city.

Some citizens clamor for control of this overpopulation. They do not want the begging dogs on the streets any longer. But previous attempts to curb the population by sterilization or culling have met with failure, as few want to adopt neutered animals. So, the dogs remain.

"In Moscow there are all sorts of stray dogs. But there are no stupid dogs," says Alexei Vereshchagin, a biologist who has spent years observing and studying the phenomenon of feral dogs in Moscow.

He remarks that though there are not a great number of dogs on the subway system —perhaps only five hundred— they have gotten quite a bit of notoriety. As we have seen from Malchik's example, people have mixed feelings about the dogs. Dogs stay out of the way of the commuters rushing to get to work on time. They approach people who are not in a hurry.

Amazingly enough, there are several dogs that take the train to specific stops independent of any human assistance. Vereshchagin claims that they appear to go where they had good luck in the past with a certain person.

"No self-respecting feral dog would bother to rise from a lying position to beg (on the train). But as soon as the occasional slow-moving elderly lady that fed you last week comes by, you eagerly wag your tail and appear interested in her problems.

"In fact, for a dog it is worth riding the bus system once a week just to get to this one person, if she has your interests at heart."

Alexei notes that if the dogs are travelling in packs, they will send the cutest, smallest dog in the pack to receive handouts. In addition, they have adopted the method of having a small pack follow a distracted person, not trying to bite them or harm him in anyway, but then issuing a loud bark to cause the unsuspecting human to drop his meal, leaving it for the hungry pack to devour.

Vereschagin remarks further that he has noted dogs obeying traffic signals, even when it is the dead of night or when the dog is not waiting for other people to cross. Since they have the type of eyesight that does not allow color perception, Vereschagin posits that the dogs learn the position of the light when they need to cross.

Further, he believes that individual dogs learn the sound of the name of the particular bus stop where they need to exit. There may be accompanying smells to the station also. In any case, the animals appear confident when they exit the bus; they do not turn back to question their decision to leave.

"Dogs go out of their way to get along with humans. Public defecation is rare. Many people choose to feed them, and some even build basic shelters for them. They are a component of the city's character."

When they first became an aspect of the city's character is a matter for speculation. Vladimir Gilyarovsky, a journalist famous for writing about Moscow's poverty and crime in the mid eighteen-hundreds wrote about the stray dogs. They had already become a self-perpetuating phenomenon, said by some to protect the city from wild animals that would otherwise enter the city proper.

As already touched upon, these feral animals are not subject to selective breeding by people who want a certain body type or conformation. In fact, any influences of human behavior on this large population are minimal. These are not dogs trying to move toward domestication. In fact, scientist Dr. Poyarkov believes that the Muscovite pool of dogs represent tiers of canine societies moving from domestication to wildness.

One group has adopted a guard dog mentality. The packs that form this group are supplied with food and encouraged to stick around businesses that need protection from unwanted intruders, such as factories, warehouses, and hospitals. These dogs are allied with a 'master' at the business they protect, therefore these dogs growl and bark viciously when someone walks by. If the person is on the other side of the street, especially if that person has a dog, the feral dog will cross the street to threaten them.

The guard dog's physical appearance is not different from any other feral dog. That is, they do not look like a German Shepherd Dog, Doberman Pinscher or other recognizable guard dog breed. Territoriality appears to be innate in this class, and he or she makes it clear that there is to be no trespassing on her turf.

Another subset of feral dogs, the beggar class, has no personal association with anyone but spend most of their waking hours around people. They do not wag their tails or jump up on people, and view them merely as a walking food source. Poyarkov says, "These beggars are excellent psychologists. These dogs not only smell who is carrying something tasty, but sense which people will stop and feed them."

The third group comprises dogs that have very little to do with people and interact basically only with other strays. Their main strategy for acquiring food is gathering scraps from the streets and the many open rubbish bins. Neither of these two groups is hostile to people, nor do they particularly try to ingratiate themselves.

The final group is composed of wild dogs. "There are dogs living in the city that are not socialized to people. They know people, but view them as dangerous. Their range is extremely broad, and they are predators. They catch mice, rats and the occasional cat. They live in the city, but out of the way of most people, therefore as a rule near industrial complexes, or in wooded parks. They are nocturnal and walk about when there are fewer people on the streets."

This is the population which is most fearsome. It is comprised partly of 'status' dogs that are in their first few months or years of being abandoned by their owner. Usually these dogs are abandoned because of their uncontrolled aggressiveness. Recent reports highlight high and rising levels of dog attacks. Over eight thousand attacks in the past few years have been serious enough to need medical attention, and there was one fatality. These attacks are usually in forested areas among dogs that are poorly socialized to human beings to begin with, and are in contrast to the feral dogs. These aggressive dogs have not established territories, and may viciously fight each other for dominance.

As opposed to these abandoned status dogs, strays that were born feral appear to be held in check by Moscow's available food and shelter. It has been estimated that only 3% of puppies survive the grueling conditions. Survival statistics are not known for the animals that are dumped into the general population of strays.

Efforts to control the ferals by the city have failed miserably. Dog catchers and sterilization campaigns have made no significant dent in the stray dog population. In addition, some Muscovites look at neutering as a crippling procedure. No one wants neutered animals.

For better or worse, the thirty-five thousand dogs appear to be a fact of life and one that Malchik's aggressor aside, many cherish. They nourish them, rely on them for protection of their property, and believe Moscow would not be the same without them.

CHAPTER SEVEN

DOGS AS BROTHERS

A true story of unique demands on a dog pack.

The four-year-old boy rounds the corner of the treacherous street. Icicles hang heavily from the buildings near downtown. The days are dark, brutish, and short. Moscow in the dead of winter seems as inhospitable as Siberia.

He fails to yield when cars barrel through the intersection, and he is caught off guard and stumbles.

Three dogs follow close behind him.

The animals are not aware of the boy's youth, and though adults that pass may cast a glance at him, they do not stop to lend a hand.

Any boy that has dogs with him cannot be lost.

The boy backs away from the intersection, scrounges in the trash cans near him, and pulls out an object wrapped in paper, which he promptly eats. The dogs sniff him and pull closer as he discards the wrapper on the sidewalk. They fight over the paper. The boy digs deeper in the trash, pulls out other refuse, and drops it for the dogs.

Then they make their way across the street, avoiding the intersection this time. The boy spends some time looking in shop windows, then moves to the next intersection. On the group progresses with its pattern: looking through refuse, eating, fighting over scraps, moving along.

Occasionally the group contacts or interacts with other packs. Ivan's is the only pack which contains a human being. The dogs, unlike wild wolves, allow the interaction of the members as long as they are in neutral territory.

The boy finds a single glove and puts it on. He enters a recessed doorway, curls up with the dogs, and endures a fitful sleep.

When the child awakes, it is still night. He is shivering, and his stomach feels empty. There is dog hair covering his inadequate clothing, evidence of the pack warming his frail body during the minus 27 degree cold.

The boy scans the nearby buildings. He prefers the downtown area for its relative ease of finding scraps of discarded food. But the chance of being captured is much greater.

Only six weeks ago, the authorities cornered him and his dogs against a building in the downtown area, and they fought viciously to protect his life.

He stood at the rear of the group of dogs, snarling and showing his teeth, and then slipped away when his pack attacked the police officers. As the dogs' canine teeth contacted bone, crimson blood flowed, and the officers let the boy go.

His name is Ivan Mishukov. Born into a family where the only adult male is an alcoholic, he can no longer live with the screams and beatings, and at four years old, he leaves home to live with a pack of dogs.

It is easy for him to be accepted.

He feeds the dogs scraps of food, and is non-threatening.

How did the boy know that living with a pack of dogs

would be preferable to living with alcoholic humans? There is no record that he earlier possessed a dog. Maybe he just stumbled on this source of spiritual acceptance, love, and protection when all he had wanted to do was die. The pack rose above the worldly torment he had received and provided a different sort of answer to his search for sanity.

Further, they provide the warmth of their bodies and the protection of their snarls, and perfect rows of slashing teeth.

Ivan eventually becomes the pack's leader, and no other dogs are allowed within his circle. He learns to pant when he is tired of running, jump over obstacles with four feet, and carry game in his mouth. His senses sharpen. He can sense danger, and it always seems that it comes from the human sector.

One morning, the child makes his way to a heap of rubble in a less populous area of the city. There is barbed wire and some other barriers that he ignores. He needs rest, but he is weak from days of starvation. The dogs had provided no food for him either, and all had hungry bellies.

Homeless people had set up an encampment here, and there was fire and shelter and the smell of food enhancing his dizziness. Their interaction may have gone something like this.

Ivan approached them in the role of a boy, a role as unfamiliar to him as though he were trying to fly. Having lost the ability to speak his native tongue, he used the universal gesture of holding out his hand. The man he approached shooed the dogs away, and Ivan retaliated by growling and showing his unimpressive deciduous teeth.

The hobo burst into laughter, holding onto his abdomen and laughing at the wee, filthy, intense lad.

"You, you wish to threaten me?" the man said, laughing again.

Then he turned his back to the boy and motioned to some of the other folks near him.

"This boy is trying to pretend he has canine blood," he said. The other humans gathered around him.

"Now maybe the police will have something to say to him when they get ahold of him."

"Yeah, let's blow the whistle, and the police will come running to help!"

Everyone except the boy put forth with thunderous laughter.

"Come here, dogs, I'll feed you with my boot," said the first man.

Ivan and the pack left with ferocious barking.

The pack went hungry that night.

The next day marked a pivotal point in the child's life. Someone besides the homeless people had apparently spied the unlikely quartet struggling to survive. Perhaps they had seen his clothing, more appropriate for a season earlier, or that he had no adult with him.

Whatever the reason, the authorities decided to take another chance to capture the child. They placed bait in the front of a restaurant after hours in the area that the boy frequented, and ensured that the dogs would follow the scent inside.

Ivan reportedly snarled, barked, clawed and fought back viciously, but eventually was subdued.

He was six years old.

The authorities said that in the two years he was feral, he lived the life of a half-boy, half-dog.

There are those that disagree. From his birth, he was treated like a cur by those who he was supposed to trust. He made the decision at the ripe age of four to turn from this type of humanity to a richer, more loving form of life as a dog. Accepted, even revered as pack leader, he lived the life of a dog. His struggles to eat, feed and clothe himself were preferable to his life as a human.

I submit that he was all dog. Yes, he had the human capacity to reach into the refuse bin or calculate traffic complexities, but there was no lingering flirtation with being human again.

He adopted the spirit of the dog.

His re-integration into society was slow, and took place in fits and starts.

He had no memory of his native language, though he had spoken at one time and thus was able to earn it more quickly than a totally naive subject.

He had no manners, and was totally lacking in social graces. But like his canine teachers, he was quick-witted, courageous, persistent, clever, loyal and able. In other words, he had superlative character.

Return to the society and people he had shunned was a lengthy and painful pursuit. He preferred to run on all fours to cover any distance, and rebelled against the prospect of walking upright when he was startled or needed to make tracks. The action of his tongue, so accustomed to snarls and clicks, was slow to accept the cadence of words.

In any situation where he felt trapped or surrounded, he responded like a wild animal.

By fits and starts, he returned to life in society, but he appeared to have a lot of regrets. Pack life with dogs offered him a fulfilling life for a significant portion of his formative years, apparently providing a spiritual connection unavailable from his humans. The degree of angst he must have felt at four years of age is incalculable. How could he step back into society?

As is clear from his history, he was tenacious and clever.

Guarded, reluctant observation of other humans whose treatment was entirely different from his parents nudged him back to the human race.

Eventually he studied voraciously, as though he could never get filled. He became a scholar.

Much later he gave interviews.

His loyalty led him to eventually serve in the Russian army.

Does he miss his previous identity and companions? I was unable to find the answer to this question.

CHAPTER EIGHT

FOXES AS DOGS

A courageous Soviet scientist persists in his drive to seek a genetic basis for tameness in animals despite the risk of being put to death. This tale relates some of the surprising side effects of domestication.

Dmitry Belyaev lives a lie.

It starts out innocently enough. He and his older brother Nikolay are intrigued about the behavior of dogs, specifically wondering how domestication altered them. Most importantly, they want to know if these mysterious changes involve genetics. They are fascinated by the profound modifications that appeared when wolves' wild nature was interfered with and they became domesticated dogs. Studying these physical and behavioral refinements is the brothers' goal.

It is hard to overstate the danger to Soviet geneticists during the 1930s. Darwin's theories are being described as "fake science." A group of non-geneticists are putting forth a popular theory stating that there is no limit to what can be manipulated; that rye can be turned into wheat under the right conditions. None other than Joseph Stalin stands up from his seat and claps when these theories are touted, while his henchmen arrest and put on trial several geneticists for treason.

Two stories circulate about what happened to Nikolay Belyaev. One states that he is sent to Siberia to a hard-labor camp where he later died. Another says he was arrested and assassinated without a trial in the late 1930s.

Meanwhile Dmitry, younger than his brother by sixteen years but no less avid a geneticist, procures a position directly out of college at the Department of Fur Bearing Animals. Knowing the stakes, he disguises his research as physiology, the study of the processes of the body. Therein is the lie.

His research convinces him that changes become visible at the tiniest biological level when any creature becomes tamed. He believes that molecules are permanently transformed when an animal becomes domesticated. Much like the pickle which can never become a cucumber again, the animal is altered to a slightly different creature.

Dmitry, alone in his work and without any access to gene sequencing or other sophisticated methods, is nevertheless certain that his brother would want him to pursue this study of metamorphosis. Within a short time, he realizes that his only option is to mimic nature's processes using an animal that has never been domesticated: the silver fox.

During the coldest winter in one of the most dreaded locales on earth, Dmitry Belyaev kneels and stretches forth his hand to a fox. They both live in Siberia, on the grounds of a camp with little chance of escape, at least for the fox. For Belyaev, he has made this freezer his new home.

The fox throws himself against the side of his kennel toward Belyaev, whining and begging for attention. He rolls on his back for a belly rub, and chortles his pleasure as he is stroked. Belyaev, apparently lost in the moment, abandons himself to the pleasure his tamed fox brings.

Dimitry begins his new experiment in 1957, thoroughly convinced of a genetic angle to domestication. His associate in the experiment, Lyudmila Trut, then a graduate student, makes the rounds of fur farms to adopt over 100 female and male foxes that might otherwise be destroyed. These animals are not wild, having spent some time in cages, but they are far from tame. Belyaev puts together a long-term breeding program to test his theories about ways in which domestication changes the fox.

Dimitry sets up a protocol using only one criteria: both male and female of any mating pair must be receptive to human beings, if only mildly so. In other words, the foxes are not sought out because of any physical dimension. He wants to find out if he can eventually produce a domesticated wild animal.

It is very difficult at first to remain aloof because many of the young foxes are so petrified at the approach of humans that they cower and growl, plastering themselves against the far side of their cages. Yet the observers have an important job to do. Their monthly session determines if the kits will accept people. Volunteers answer a series of questions on every fox's behavior toward them and other foxes. One of the questions is whether the fox prefers the company of other foxes, or that of human beings. The researcher takes a long minute to see if the fox grows calmer, or if there are any signs that it will accept handheld food. The vast majority of these animals refuse food and recoil at the approach of humans.

Dmitry decides to take the most approachable 20% of the females and a slightly smaller percentage of the males to mate. He is careful that the study separates any animals that are related, to remove the chance of any interbred offspring.

Not surprisingly, the foxes tend to become tamer. Belyaev categorizes his foxes into three groups depending on their responsiveness to people. Class III are the least responsive to people. Class II allow some human contact, but do not relish it. Class I enjoys human contact.

After only six generations, a fourth category is established to include those animals which lick the volunteers, whine at their approach, and allow play. Currently, after forty years of selective breeding and 45,000 foxes, upwards of seventy percent behave similarly to the one playing with Dimitry.

After this time has elapsed, the foxes also look different. The male's faces and skulls tended to become more 'feminized,' with smaller braincases and shorter snouts. The colors of their fur changes, from dark silver to brownish-red or sandy in shade. Their tails turn up, and in some cases, tail vertebrae were actually lost from one generation to the next. White markings appear on the head or chest. These physical events link the taming gene with many other seemingly unrelated genes.

Belyaev's observations do not stop with physical characteristics or behavioral changes. He analyzes the foxes' blood stream also. He is fascinated to see whether the animals' stress level changes after generations in captivity. By design, he harnesses foxes that had already gone through the rigors of capture and caging, so when he moved them to his farm, they were already somewhat less wild. But he was shocked to see that even after a few generations, their cortisol level (a stress hormone) dropped, and continues to drop over time. The foxes' stress levels drop the longer they are in captivity. While this is occurring, neurotransmitters increase.

Dimitry hypothesizes that these profound changes come

about because an individual fox's genetic code changes when they are domesticated. He believes that all the genes he studies are linked. He demonstrates that neurotransmitter genes cooperate with taming genes which in turn coordinate with color-causing genes. Thus, as the little fox's genes combine in successive generations, there are new color combinations or new tail lengths as the genetic material shows up in a unique way.

It is tantalizing to note that Frank Albert, who was for a time continuing Dmitry's work, found several key regions of the genome that have a strong effect on tameness and that he suspects the involvement of "at least half a dozen genes" that contribute to an animal's tameness. The next step is "to locate individual genes that influence tameness and aggression."

Of course, this is not a book about the life of foxes, but it is about domestication and the changes that take place in animals when they have gone through succeeding generations under the selective breeding of man.

Dimitry's half-century long experiment shows us that in the short span of one person's lifetime, under the correct circumstances, domestication of the fox can and does occur.

This is tremendously fast.

This could have happened with dogs.

Given the right circumstances involving a group of prehistoric humans that are motivated, similar changes can unfold. And if, as some current researchers believe, wolves sought out humans, taming may have taken place within a scant few human generations.

Because I am examining multiple theories for how dogs and humans became co-domesticated, I thought it interesting to observe that a similar taming procedure could have happened in the Yangtze River area 16,000 years ago. The wolf tamers likely have clearly these principles.

THE SOUL OF MY WORK

Following are stories I have collected, mostly from my veterinary patients or personal pets that I find exceptional. Close to my heart, they give me a brief taste of what my client's life is like.

We share a moment as clear as any crystal.

CHAPTER NINE

DOG AS SPIRITUAL BEING

The day I meet Jaspar, little did I know his story would change my life.

W et from the rain, monstrous in proportions, it is the Cocker's owner who initially commands attention. The drizzle has not been kind to her. Thinning hair toppling down the sides of her face, the unflattering dress and weary shoes do nothing to encourage my sensitive receptionist, Janey.

The client perches herself on the reception counter. "I demand an appointment now." It is the end of an emotionally and physically exhausting day.

I exchange glances with Janey, who is backing away in her swivel chair. "Have you been here before?"

"He's never been sick before. Today he is." Her rhythmic chewing indicates that the gum in her mouth is still satisfactory.

"What seems to be the trouble?" Janey asks in a halting voice.

The client adjusts her bulbous weight to lean closer to the woman waiting on her. "He's got a lump," she says, "on his head." Then she leans back with the satisfied air of someone who has done her job well.

Janey takes some notes and then turns to her computer, casting a sidelong look of desperation at me. I nod.

"Please come right in," Janey says with relief.

The woman lumbers down the hallway, a satchel over her shoulder. The handbag is squirming.

"What can I help you with today?" Without consciously thinking about it, I feel complete confidence in my ability to handle whatever situation presents itself. After all, I have thirty years experience with suffering animals.

"This is what you can help me with," she says, wrinkling her nose either at my haughtiness or the dog's condition. Out of her knapsack she delivers the rear end, then the forequarters of a dog, about twenty-five pounds of him. Covering his body are streaks of dirt and blood and unmentionable goo. The smile on my face begins to fade. When I see the tumor on his head, I am truly horrified. Very little skin remains to cover its grey expanse. His pain is intense. Besides the scratch marks on the growth itself, his left eye is scratched and ulcerated as well.

Attempting to cover the flip flopping of my unprepared stomach, I turn to look directly into the client's eyes.

"Please let me draw up an injection of pain medication for your dog...what is his name...Jaspar?" I methodically fan out the intake papers on my countertop.

She says, "Where were you when I needed you last week?"

I look again directly into her eyes. "Excuse me? Needed me?" Fumbling for further words and trying to review my whereabouts the last seven days, I use the only trick I know. Examine her eyes to gauge where the situation is going.

Apparently dropping that subject entirely, she pulls a roll of bills from the handbag.

She holds the money out to me. "He's suffered enough. He got sick when I was on a cruise with my sister and you weren't around to help. So, I need to know what it's going to cost me to put him to rest."

"Can I recommend an oncologist? They have amazing treatments…"

She interrupts me. "He's not going to live long enough to see an oncologist. Why would I put him through that? Treatments and surgery and pain all by himself. He doesn't know what life is like without me. That's why he fell apart when I was gone. And now he has to be put to sleep."

I put on a pair of exam gloves and walk close to Jaspar, patting and stroking him for a long minute and keenly feel my inability to make him recover. Usually when this happens, I have the wherewithal to squelch it and move on. But with increasing frequency, an awareness about my powerlessness in the face of disease has been haunting me.

"If this is your decision, I need you to sign a consent form, and I'll let the receptionist know that you are ready to pay. Then my staff members will place an intravenous catheter, so everything will be smooth."

I take Jaspar to the treatment area, restraining him against my lab coat. I present him to my technical staff and trudge to the narcotics box for the pain medication and final injection. When I return to Jaspar's guardian I find that she wants to hold him on her lap. I kneel below her and cup his arm to administer the drug. A very emotional procedure up to this point, and unfortunately very familiar.

However, this is not to be routine for me, and I don't know if it ever will be again. The reason is that for the first time in my career, I see Jaspar's spirit leave him.

Once a whole dog with serious medical problems, he becomes something else. The organs and systems that support his life stop. They don't wind down slowly; they come to an abrupt halt. His pupils dilate and don't return to normal. They are wide open in the most extraordinary way, as though willing me to stare into their depths where there are no longer any secrets.

His head is flexible on his owner's lap; there is no muscle tone to keep him rigid any longer.

I am a witness that moments earlier he was imbued with a life force so rich that it orchestrated all the functions of his body. That force evaporates. I see an ethereal form exiting his body. It leaves through his eyes, wispy like a dream, with a short white tail of dew. Then it is gone.

After proper hugs and goodbyes, I excuse myself from the room and closet myself in my office. There I call one of my closest colleagues.

"Yes," he assures me, "I have experienced the same evaporation of life repeatedly during my career."

"Why didn't I get it before?" I ask him.

He says merely, "you weren't ready."

~

This book does not assume that you are ready.
It just assumes that you are curious.

CHAPTER TEN

WOLF

A moment that caused me to vibrate at a higher harmonic than I thought possible.

I am not a doctor of wild animals. That profession is not for the faint of heart. I don't mind kneeling, or getting on the floor with a patient, but I heartily approve of proper restraint of a creature that has no qualms about making a snack of me.

It is late afternoon on a Thursday when I glance out the window at a wolf and her handler wending their way through the parking lot. The sunlight flares off the spiky fur and poofed cheeks of the beast. She takes her steps carefully, as though blacktop is too foreign to be tolerated.

Zelda does not wag her tail when she enters the exam room. She does not sniff the furniture or the floor, and she is not interested in dry biscuits.

Her handler holds the animal against his body with an air of frantic insecurity. A leather leash thick enough to subdue a tiger is clasped to an even more substantial brown harness.

A wire basket muzzle decorates her head. The tooled brown straps are interwoven behind her ears, and tightened with a metal ring.

Her nose is disfigured by drainage from an ugly festering

wound. Half the black leather part is decayed away, and she cannot fully close her mouth. Perhaps from pain.

My focus is on the proximity of her wound to the perfectly chiseled canine teeth, and their ability to puncture human flesh. No matter that she is muzzled. I don't turn my back on her.

"How long has that pus been draining?" I ask, trying to act nonchalant.

The question ringing in my ears is about how frequently this wolf has been handled by people, but I did not voice this. We are playing everything by ear. What would I do differently anyway?

"About six weeks," he says, clutching the leash impossibly close to his heart. "We think there is a piece of tooth lodged there."

The magnifying hood that I wear is a bulky, grey-colored affair that extends three or four inches off the top of my head. Trying to think like Lupus, I shift it more tightly onto my forehead, which suddenly feels overly large. Will she will find this unexpected bulge on my head to be threatening? As I sidle up to her sideways, avoiding her eyes, I see no change in her posture to signal fear, or even interest. I need no more than a brief look to see the edges of the wound flaring out, dead tissue within.

"John," I say to the handler, "If Ida lets me, I can attempt to probe the wound using a local anesthetic.

"Or I can tranquilize her and do the job more quickly with less likelihood of pain."

"Try the local first."

"OK," I said. "Let me go get it."

This means that in approximately two minutes, I will be

eyeball-to-eyeball with a wild animal, responsible for her care. It is daunting.

I draw up the lidocaine I need. For good measure, I draw up an extra dose also.

As I re-enter the room, I am struck that her coat belies her actual size, which is a little over sixty pounds. The fur makes her look seventy-five. I take my first close look at her. Her face is wedge-shaped, with copper lizard eyes, vacant expression, drooling through the muzzle. I have not seen dogs which possess the undercoat and prickly guard hairs which Zelda wears so naturally.

Walking slowly, I eventually kneel in front of the beast. I avoid eye contact, and gently touch her nose with a forefinger.

She throws her head. Maybe it is my imagination, but when her head comes to rest in a neutral position again, her expression is much less calm.

"John, I can't do this. She's not going to allow it."

"I don't want to tranquilize her. how will I know if she'll wake up OK?"

"I can't even touch her nose." I demonstrate again. This time she rears, catching him off guard, and flipping him over on his back to the ground.

"Think about it," I say, "if I tranquilize her I can radiograph her nose and make certain there is not a cracked piece of tooth in there." Then I leave the room to give him time to decide.

While my technician prepares a tranquilizer, I start the digital dental X-ray. It delivers such a high resolution fine beam, that it is my overwhelming choice for this delicate task ahead.

John looks thoughtful when I return to the room. "I didn't realize there was a science to this," he says.

I say, "I wouldn't want someone digging in my nose when

they didn't even know what they would find."

"What are you going to do with her?" he asks, kneeling by her head, leash wrapped tightly around his knuckles. He starts crying. "She's like the daughter I never had. So beautiful. So wild."

I am taken aback.

"I didn't know you felt like that," I say. I hesitate and then say, "You rely on me to be objective. That allows me take care of this wound properly so that it will heal."

I walk over to him. "She needs to get better once and for all. This isn't fair to her."

He sobs, "She's not even interested in me. She's not attached to anyone. I don't know why I love her so much." His shoulders are shaking.

"Do we choose who and why we love?" I ask. "You are around these exquisite creatures all day. You admire everything they do, and you are very involved. It's natural," I say. "Now let me fix her up. Do you want to be present when she gets her shot, or do you want to be in the other room?"

"Here," he says.

Working around the hug he has on her body, I administer the injection, once again marveling at Zelda's long fur and comparatively lean body. It is obvious that our strength would have been no match for her. I feel flabby.

Eventually Zelda's body slumps, and John's goes along.

"We need to transport her," I say to him. "I'll take the back end and guide you to the X-ray table."

Once we have her positioned, everyone is required to be out of the beam. Immediately when asked, the computerized X-ray screen shows us that within the nose there is a horseshoe-shaped curve of jagged white.

"Look," I show him, "there is a piece of enamel from another wolf's tooth lodged in her nose."

John hovers over my shoulder, and points to the ivory spicule of tooth.

"Is that it?" he asks.

I reply, "That's it. When we get that out, her troubles are over."

While one of the technicians escorts the client from the room, the other monitors the sleeping wolf's breathing and heart rate. Rectifying the damage requires a quick jerk of the wrist to remove the bit of enamel using some large hemostats, and cleanup of the putrid tissue left behind. The computer reassures me that there is no remaining tooth.

I reverse her tranquilizer. She is conscious in twenty minutes and walking in forty.

John and I have a talk. "There's a wolf in your den that has a fractured canine tooth," I say. "And given the size of that sliver, the other wolf probably needs to have its tooth capped."

"Probably the other female," he says. "They don't share."

"I'd love to come out and see them sometime."

And I never do, and he never brought the other female to the clinic, which is why I can only brag about seeing one wolf up close.

I used to reflect as to whether that wolf thought the trade off was worth it—my manipulating her consciousness, rooting around in her nose, changing the course of the natural history of her disease so that her handler and I could feel satisfied with our contribution. In Paradise, the foreign object would continue to fester until either the body rejected it, or the infection would spread. She might lose the side of her nose, have difficulty breathing, or be subject to continual low-level infections that depressed her immune system.

I consider how much chance has to do with life. Which are strong, and which are weak, which get medical care, and which don't. Especially which exit Paradise, and which remain.

CHAPTER ELEVEN

A DOG INDULGED

Too much spoiling makes a dog creative.

Mrs. and Mr. Corbett arrive a good half hour before their appointment. Their clothes are slightly behind the times and formal. He wears a hounds-tooth yellowish three-piece suit. She has on a blue and white flowered dress that flows quite a bit below her knees. Her hair has a slightly blue tinge; his is arranged carefully to cover a telltale balding spot.

They could be anyone's elderly neighbors: quiet, punctual, neat.

At Mrs. Corbett's feet, tongue extended and panting heavily is Buster, their Schnauzer. From previous experience I know that Buster has been kept up-to-date on all vaccines and testing.

The Corbetts are the perfect clients.

Buster is not; at least that is what I am being told.

"His jealousy has gotten worse and worse," says Mr. Corbett. "When he was a pup, he would whine and complain when we left the house, and sometimes pull curtains off the wall or eat up pens that were lying around."

"He especially loves plastic," says Mrs. Corbett.

"Yes, yes," says Mr. Corbett. "Of course, that is correct, if we were talking about the past. But now he goes after our clothes."

"While they are on," adds Mrs. Corbett. "While you are wearing them."

Mr. Corbett scuffs his foot along the floor and looks down at his heavily polished shoes. "I feel like I am being unfaithful talking about him this way, but I really am at a loss."

Mrs. Corbett sneaks a look at her husband. "There, there, dear, we agreed that we need to talk to the doctor, not to the floor." She leans forward in a conspiratorial manner, her hand behind her mouth to direct the words in my direction.

"He pulls off my husband's pants when he walks toward the door. At first, we thought he didn't mean to, that it was a result of his playfulness, but now he jumps at my husband's belt and shakes it like it is a snake." She makes vigorous hand motions to demonstrate.

"Well," he said, "he'll do the same thing to you if you try to leave. It's not just me. He shreds your stockings or rips out the hem of your dress if you try to leave the house first. Pokes holes in your coat."

"My wardrobe is about finished," the woman agrees.

She sighs deeply.

"But eventually, my wife concocted a plan," said Mr. Corbett. "A very good one, though it's time consuming."

Neither spoke for a moment so I waited patiently. Then, "Go on."

"If I bundle a spare change of clothing in my arms and stand at the front door, Martha has long enough to go out the back door while he is mauling me. And her clothes are unscathed."

"Then I knock at the outside of the back door and he gets

distracted while he runs to the back door, and Herman has time to get out." She grins widely.

"Then I can change my pants in the car." Herman smiles and looks pleased with the execution of Martha's plan.

I believe my smile is fading at this point as I imagine these septuagenarians trying to avoid injuring their dog's feelings about his place in the pack order.

As gently as possible, I insinuate that training of the three of them might have spectacular results and save both their skins and their remaining wardrobes.

"I like where this is going," I say. "You are very flexible with Buster and love him dearly.

"These are the two most important constituents of re-programming his mind. Training is just a gentle tweaking of his consciousness so that you are in charge and not him."

Both clients' attention seemed to wander.

"Then he won't be our Buster," said Mr. Corbett. "We want him just as he is. He has a great spirit! We thought you could help us find a good doctor to help with the scratches?"

I walked close to Mrs. Corbett so that I could grasp her hand. "I'd be happy to help you with a good doctor for your wounds. But I would also like to have someone meet with you so that you won't get scratched so often.

"Are you willing to meet with the technician that handles our behavior problems? She is very gentle. She will help us examine Buster so that we can be sure he doesn't have any health problems either, that could be making his life unhappy. Then you can take care of those issues if there is something wrong."

Both Corbetts seemed pleased with these ideas, and even Buster seemed to get on board with the physical exam and numerous treats that he received.

The clincher is that Buster had very high lipid levels in his blood and may have been experiencing periodic pancreatitis. When we found a diet that fit him better, along with a persistent and patient trainer, he greatly decreased his clothes-destroying behavior.

CHAPTER TWELVE

A DOG CHALLENGE

At times, I provide service to non-domesticated animals.

"**H**ulk's coming in today," whisper the receptionists among themselves.

"What's he here for?" I overhear.

"He's got another ear infection. His owner cannot treat him, and there's something wrong with his knee."

"Well I hope they scheduled enough time for him," someone says. "Last time, he was here all afternoon. And they couldn't get him sedated no matter what they used."

"He's coming in at eleven. No one will get lunch break today."

I am rather excited to see this infamous dog walk through the door. And when he does—double muzzled with drool coating his forelegs presumably from the car ride—I feel slightly let down.

Hulk is a rather small Chow Chow, with golden-red unkempt fur knotted behind his ears and all along his flanks from lack of acquaintance with the brush. His open eyes are nevertheless nearly covered by his eyelids, so full of curly hair and immense folds of skin on his head that only a small fissure is allowed. His mane looks as thick and impressive as a lion's, so you feel you can grab it with both hands and still have loose skin left over.

His head wanders side to side with an alligator-like precision, mapping out the territory and savoring the thought of his next victim.

"Good morning, Sir," says the receptionist. "Good morning Hulk." She nods in his general direction. "Did you give the tranquilizers that the doctor recommended?""

"Of course," says Mr. Prynn. "All three of them. They didn't do anything that I can see. They never work. I don't know why I even bother to give them, or come back here for that matter."

The receptionist smiles sweetly. "Yes, Mr. Prynn. Let me get you and Hulk in a room and then I will fetch the nurse."

Anna draws the short straw, and enters the room, standing with the exam table between her and Hulk for protection. She takes the history and comes out of the room, facing me. I have drawn the short straw also.

"He wants X-rays of the knee. He wants an exam first, though."

"Did you explain that we need to use a cocktail of sedatives first, to even be able to touch him?" I ask.

"Oh, he's aware, but unhappy."

I enter the room. "Hello Mr. Prynn. I can't examine Hulk because he won't let me touch him. Let me give him a sedative first and then I will check him over. I'll need you to leave the room so that he won't feel protective of you."

"No, I'll stay right here with him. Tell me what to do."

"We are going to use a long-distance syringe, that is a syringe on a pole to inject him. Can you hold the leash tightly?"

He nods affirmatively.

Anna comes in with the pole. I get within six feet of him, and he erupts. He bucks like a bull let out of the chute, then rolls, kicking his rear legs, biting hideously at the muzzle, and tearing the leash out of the owner's hands. He lunges for me, initially at my hands and then toward my throat. I held onto the pole for dear life, and plunge it into the inferno's shoulder, feeling it contact bone.

Hulk backs away for a moment, urinating on himself and slipping on the floor. Then he gathers all his steam and launches himself toward my face. Something thick and covered with saliva bangs into my cheek. Even though he still has the muzzle on, I fear for my safety, and I throw myself backwards out of the door, forcibly pushing Anna out ahead of me.

Hulk is lying in a heap on the floor when I return, and I wait a few extra moments before examining his chest for the heart rate. My own heart is skating, as though there are no beats fast enough to describe it. 'I must act professional' I say to myself, and I re-tighten the muzzles on his face before shakily taking culture swabs to figure out what is fulminating in Hulk's ears.

"Set up the X-ray for his knee," I instruct Anna, and she comes out with a measuring device from the radiology room. My respiratory rate has escalated during the incident, and I can hear Anna breathing noisily also.

I hold out my hand for the device and she gives it to me. I take the measurement without further incident, and she sets up the proper parameters on our equipment. The owner insists on remaining with his dog, and we let him carry Hulk all the way to the radiology room table, where he places his dog in gingerly fashion.

"We've got about ten minutes," I say. "Let's do it in five." I manipulate the joint until I am satisfied that we do have a ruptured cruciate ligament, and then *Whirrr Whirrr* the radiographs are taken, and placed on the screen for viewing.

"Good enough for a specialist," I say, then placed a dab of long-acting ear anti-infection product in both Hank's ears.

As we move Hank from the table to the floor to let him recover without falling off the radiology device, we inadvertently rouse him. Hulk brings both forefeet along the sides of his muzzle minutes earlier than I would have thought possible. In one fell swoop, both muzzles are off. Obviously still dazed, the animal nevertheless coordinates his muscles well enough to do some damage. One gets the feeling he has performed these acts of defiance many times before.

I motion Mr. Prynn back to the exam room.

"We will have him recover here in the darkroom and then you can lead him out to the car."

"OK," said Mr. Prynn. "But can you trim his toenails first?"

CHAPTER THIRTEEN

DOG WITH TERMINAL DISEASE

A gentleman teaches me that there are many ways to show courage.

I have a modest lobby, but the animal waiting for the next appointment makes everything around him look grand. He has wiry short black and tan fur, with each hair lying perfectly in its place as though a tailor of dog's coats had taken special care with this one. A stub of a tail stays erect to monitor which way the wind blows. His body is black and sleek, with a deep chest reserved for those large breeds that must propel wind in and out of heavily muscled ribs.

But the eyes. To say that they are soft is to do them a genuine disservice. Brown yes; intelligent yes; but also deep and sensitive; concerned; self-aware.

Baci is a long-legged Doberman Pinscher, a troubled patient from the look of his owner and the obvious swelling at the animal's shoulder and neck. It is clear from the dog's expression that he has come here to be diagnosed and treated. Every arresting millimeter of him from his claws to his pointed ears indicates stoicism mixed with curiosity. And pain. Unremitting pain.

"Come in Baci. Come in Chris." I invite him and his male owner to the plushily padded chairs in the largest room of my hospital patient area. "Please sit down. Would you like some water?"

Chris waves the nicety away with his free hand.

"Baci has been lethargic, only a few days."

"Yes, I know how well you care for him," I say, as his eyes avert themselves from me. Does he need a tissue, I ponder, and thus I reach behind me to the shelving that contains such things.

"Not only lethargic, but the lumps started growing the day before yesterday. They are all over his body. Here," he pulls the one under his lower jaw toward me and I kneel besides the still animal.

I palpate it. It is firm, turgid actually; with similar pressure to a grape or a water balloon ready to burst.

I gently run my hands over the stationary animal. Bulges meet my hands behind both knees, in the groin, under the arms, and in front of the shoulders. I wrack my brains before speaking to consider anything to confer a shred of hope to this client.

"These are his lymph nodes, Chris," I say in a low tone, while touching the man's wrist which is steadying the animal.

"I know that!" he says, standing up in an agitated manner, and grabbing his short blond hair near its roots. "Of course, it's his lymph nodes. You are supposed to give me information I don't already have!"

He begins pacing, moving to within an inch of the door, and when whirling around continues to fidget with his hair till he nearly collides with the exam table. There is precious little room to maneuver in the confined space.

I get him a tissue and ask him if he needs a moment alone with Baci. He replies with a second wave of the hand, and then pounds the table with his fists. "It's lymphoma, isn't it?'

"I need to perform some tests, but yes, it is likely cancer of the lymphatic system."

"He's only five years old," the man spits out. "Why not some dog that deserves it?"

I touch his hand again as he makes this statement. I know he would never wish this on any other animal. "Chris, let me send you to a very caring doctor that only treats this kind of illness." I venture into delicate territory here, but am certain that a specialist was the best doctor to be involved in the difficult processes of evaluation and treatment.

"Or please, take your time so that you can go home and think this over."

Chris nodded his head, paid his bill for the office call, and left.

Within a week, he chooses us to begin the work of determining whether Baci is riddled with cancer and how to treat him.

Chris drops him off at the curb after imploring one of the veterinary technicians to meet him, and we work with Baci to get answers. Our answers might not have been as targeted and useful as they now are, because this was thirty years ago, but I am fresh out of school with a lot of contacts at university, and a treatment plan comes into fruition to attack Baci's lymphoma.

Various tablets are prescribed for Baci to take regularly. These lyse the abnormal cells in the lymph nodes.

But the mainstay, the big guns if you will, are injections. And Baci receives one of the most lethal of all.

Named Adriamycin, this intently colored orange liquid has the capacity to melt surrounding tissue if even a tiny drop leaks out of the vein. In school I witnessed a dog's foreleg, grey and lifeless as a cadaver's. Multiple dilutions of fluid could not dilute or repair what one drop of Adriamycin had produced.

To say that we place a catheter in Baci's leg cautiously is a gross understatement. His leg is shaved and sterilized and a nick incision performed over the bulging portal to his circulation. The catheter penetrates the vein and inches forward into position, where it is secured with various medical tapes and then checked for patency with sterile saline flushes.

Finally, with assurances all around that no damage can be done, we hang the indifferent glass receptacle containing the Adriamycin, and position our patient in a comfortable way during the delicate treatment. We are lucky to have a special patient, who lifts his nose long enough to sniff the bottle, and then twists to position his neck alongside his opposite chest wall so that his involved arm is never in danger of being tweaked.

The orange chemotherapy flows like spring runoff, coursing through the cephalic vein to the vena cava to the surging heart, and out to each lymphatic in the body. I imagine its course as clearly as though the vessels were lighting up, targeting and lysing those tumor cells.

Of course, there is fallout. As with every chemotherapeutic drug, innocent bystander tissues are blasted. White blood immunological cells and clotting agents are destroyed, and further blood tests must be conducted to determine if and when the wonder drug has overstepped its bounds.

But that is not today's work.

Today is a labor of love.

After his initial settling, Baci does not change position, stretch, or yawn.

The young women who assisted him through his chemotherapy gently escort him off the table after his treatment. Chris comes in to greet him.

Chris remarks, "He doesn't look as bad as I thought." The margins of his eyes are edged with red. His usually impeccable hair is quite tousled.

His hands shake as he holds out the MasterCard for payment.

"Chris," I say, tenderly, "he is the best patient I have ever had." I am tempted to again touch the grieving man, but his body language says 'no.'

Baci is led out to the lovely car that his owner drives, with the technicians giving instructions as they go along.

"Chris didn't say a word," they reported. "Not a syllable."

We watch as Chris assists his regal dog into the vehicle's passenger seat and places a harness across his chest. One of the young women says, "I haven't worked with Dobermans before. Isn't he incredible?"

We consent.

~

Every three weeks Baci returns for his blood test, physical exam and treatment. His blood cells waver around low normal, and he is considered to be safe to treat.

By now, Chris brings a fruit basket or a box of specialty chocolates for those participating in Baci's medical care. Baci cannot participate in chocolate eating for obvious reasons, but he always graciously accepts fruit.

His lymph nodes appear to be responding well, but Chris indicates that Baci has had several episodes of vomiting and diarrhea.

"Usually between the end of the first and beginning of the

second week." Chris appears unconcerned. Up to this point, Baci has suffered through three injections and is, as always, immobile throughout.

Today when I walk into the room where the technicians are taking vital signs, I note that something appears amiss. Baci's head is held high for the exam, and he is gracious as always. I scratch the top of his head and lift his left foreleg in preparation for placing the cephalic catheter.

In the most gentlemanly way, he raises his right foreleg and places it on top of my hand, blocking access to the other leg.

I am taken aback. The technicians both look at me. Baci is looking directly at me, a flame within his eyes. It is unmistakable.

"Go get Chris please," I instruct the technician. "I need to talk to him."

"And let's get Baci off the table." I could feel sobs welling out of my chest.

"He's going home."

CHAPTER FOURTEEN

DOGS AS EYES

This dog used his service guidebook as a doorstop.

Brenda reaches out to steady herself against a wall as she enters my office. The large puppy beside her continually steps on her feet, pushes his way in front of her, and generally makes a nuisance of himself.

Brenda, a smartly dressed young woman with sensible shoes and a diminutive red hat looks toward me pleadingly, "My dog won't use the curb when he goes to the bathroom."

She points to the young black Labrador Retriever. He bestows several heartfelt licks on my left hand before I laugh and pull away.

"What's his name?" I ask her.

"Well the Blind Association named him Jeff, but that's a man's name. I re-named him Blackie."

"Good name, good name," I encourage her. "And how old is he?"

"Eighteen months," she said. "He's been through the complete training program," she says, a look of exasperation on her face. "He knows all the commands. But he follows his own drummer."

I examine the magnificent young animal. He is the stocky

squat English variety of Lab, with a boxy face and short, powerful legs. His webbed feet look perfectly suited for swimming.

She elaborates, "The San Francisco office has puppies in training for twelve months. They learn how to walk on harness, how to negotiate traffic, and how to use the curb so that owners do not have to try to find their mess.

"I can't see it, so I can't remove it and dispose of it properly.

"When I flew out to San Francisco for the bonding session, he performed perfectly. But ever since we have come home, he refuses to use the curb, so I am left with the often-futile gesture of trying to figure out how to clean up someone else's lawn."

"What command do you give him?" I say.

She looks directly at where the dog should be, on her left side. "Blackie, curb," she replies. Blackie looks up expectantly from directly behind her, then flops down to the ground.

"How does he perform off-harness?" I ask.

"He is a mischievous little puppy. He pulls plants out of the pots and drags them across the floor. He tries to surf the counter. He drinks out of the toilet if I forget to put the top down."

I visualize this in my mind's eye, normal typical puppy behavior that nearly everyone experiences with a growing canine.

"Do you think that he has a loving spirit?" I ask. "Or do you think he is mean-spirited?"

"No, no, no," she says. "He is not mean-spirited. But I think he is suitable for a family, not for me."

"Brenda, can we run all this by the Blind Foundation? How can we get him to be a suitable companion, or better yet, a suitable assistant?"

After several minutes of tense discussion, we each agree to a task. She is willing to call the Blind Foundation, and I am willing to call another client who is blind and uses a guide dog. Her husband is also blind and uses a cane, and I feel they would be a wonderful match for her as she accustoms herself to her boisterous puppy.

My other client Susan seems thrilled that I asked her to help. "Remember when my new female lab ate her entire harness, twice?"

Of course I did. I had placed the mischievous nine-month-old puppy on the X-Ray machine myself, and seen the harness studs glinting merrily on the radiograph.

Susan and I had some oh's and ah's about that. Her dog had jumped from the floor to the bed and from there up on the dresser where he had grabbed the harness while her owner was still sleeping.

"I don't want to have you perform surgery," she told me at the time. So, I fed the pup a half loaf of bread to coat her stomach and induced her to throw everything up.

The harness wasn't even harmed.

"You're the perfect person," I say to Susan. "She needs encouragement."

We all meet at the clinic over some lively chatter, and Susan maneuvers Brenda on a short demonstration around the circumference of the parking lot.

They quickly return. "It seems that Blackie likes to be on the right side, and not the left side. If he walks that way, he curbs perfectly," Susan says.

"But that isn't the way he was trained," chimes in Brenda. "He likes to be naughty."

"Let's walk with him between us," Susan says.

"Yeah," says Brenda. "There has to be someone one his right and someone on his left. We'll switch up his brain, and then show him the right way again."

Within a week they had retrained him to use the bathroom Brenda's way. Not that they got all the mischief out so easily.

CHAPTER FIFTEEN

DOG AS SAVIOR

It doesn't matter the size of the dog; what matters is the size of the heart in the dog.

Jenny is a fourteen-year-old Pug, who sits plump and sassy on the exam room table, elastic stabilizing a fuchsia bow over each ear. Those ears are the reason she has come to the doctor.

"They are so smelly," says the elderly woman on the other side of the exam table. Mrs. McLain wags her index finger at the recalcitrant pet. "She won't let me touch her," she says.

Because they are so bothersome, I must tease the painful ears back over Jenny's head to look at the little ear canals. Throbbingly red and definitely odorous, they finally yield to gentle pressure.

Thick mustard-colored ooze coats the inner walls.

"Mrs. McLain," I say, "I would like to get you an estimate for a sedative so that Jenny will be in less pain, and we can clean her ears thoroughly."

"I know she needs medication, doctor, but what about the dangers of anesthetics?" The woman starts rooting around in her handbag, perhaps for a handkerchief.

I attempt to comfort her. "We will employ a trusted, mild tranquilizer. Without it, because of the degree of pain she is experiencing, I don't think that I can do a thorough job." I choose my next words carefully. "Everything has a risk. You have to weigh the risk of the sedative against the throbbing pain and infection she is experiencing."

After several minutes musing about the alternatives for Jenny's care, Ms. McLain states, "I am just so afraid of losing her, just so afraid of losing her." A handkerchief materializes in her timeworn hand to gently dab at the flow coming from her eyes.

I straighten up so that I can listen better. "You are worried about the sedative?"

"She saved my life, you know," says Jenny's owner. "In a fire."

By now I am listening intently and scrutinizing her face. There are long wrinkles from the edges of her eyes to her temples, and similarly deep ones along her chin. Her face seems more open and her intelligent eyes seem to be seeing the incident again.

"I am in bed, in my nightgown, fast asleep. Jenny will not stop barking, even though I keep telling her to stop.

"She gets up on the bed, which she has never done before or since. She continues to lick my face and whine until I force myself awake and come to attention enough to see that fumes are boiling out of the bathroom.

"I grab the nearest towel to extinguish the fire, but as soon as I get close to the bathroom, I realize I am no match for the inferno of smoke; I hack and bend over while my eyes feel like they are being broiled. Jenny continues to tug on my nightgown the whole time until I relent and fumble outside. My condo becomes incinerated before the fire department arrives.

"Without Jenny, neither of us would be here." Moisture drizzles from the sides of her eyes as she squeezes them shut and reaches over to grasp Jenny to her diminutive frame. Jenny's expansive grin accentuates the story.

Mrs. McLain adjusts the elastic that holds the bows in place. "I've been selfish, so selfish. I wanted my comfort more than her own. I didn't want to face the fact of her aging, the fact of her ear pain. I wanted it all to go away."

Mrs. McLain faces away from me with her Jenny. "Please get me the estimate," she says in a low voice. "But I will pay whatever it takes to get her out of pain.

"She saved my life."

CHAPTER SIXTEEN

DOG FEROCIOUS

Gentle when stroked.

Within the confines of the Denver neighborhood where I lived, there is a magnificent park that is dog friendly. Dogs of all shapes and sizes with all manner of people stroll through the gardens or lap each other on the running track that circumnavigates the park.

There is an unwritten rule that the dogs visiting the park are peaceable both with each other and with the humans seeking a pleasant experience of nature.

This rule cannot be easily enforced.

The first offense can be fatal.

That is why I was concerned when my visibly distraught neighbor who owns an intact male adult Irish Wolfhound sought my advice on a crisp autumn day.

"I took Gareth to City Park today," he said. Gareth weighs more than two hundred pounds and stands over seven feet tall when his front feet are planted on his master's shoulders.

The Wolfhound gets its name from its use as a wolf hunter and warrior, not just from its imposing appearance.

"He was fine for two thirds of the way around the lake, ignoring other dogs and people. Then suddenly this smaller dog began barking at him and getting in his face. Gareth tried to ignore him, but the other dog blocked his path.

"Gareth picked him up by the nape of his neck, arched his back like a whip, and threw him over his shoulder.

"The dog landed on the ground and I think it was still breathing, but the owner was hysterical and wouldn't let me get near his dog.

"People parted ways around us as though we were criminals. I could sense genuine fear from everyone who witnessed it, but they didn't interfere with us because I think they were certain they would be next."

I studied my neighbor. I had seen him purchase this Wolfhound and then another, a female, almost as large as the male. I knew Wolfhounds were an ancient breed, meant to clear Scotland of the scourge of wolves in the middle ages. For all their size, they are generally placid animals, but they have been used in battle.

There is a saying about them that they are "gentle when stroked, fierce when provoked."

"Dan," I said, "these animals, this breed, consists of independent thinkers. What may strike you or me as a minor offense could be considered a threat to him. Even with training, you cannot be guaranteed of a behavioral change sufficient to make him non-aggressive. Take him to a behaviorist, see what their suggestions are."

I gave him references to three local behaviorists.

Curious, I researched the breed further that night. There is a fascinating legend surrounding the gift from King John of England to Llewelyn, Prince of Wales. The ruler gave an Irish Wolfhound named Gelert to Llewelyn in 1210, and this dog became the Prince's favored dog for hunting.

One day when the Prince left for the hunt, he could not find Gelert, and he left with the other dogs, much to his displeasure.

He came home early as the hunt was unsatisfactory, and was greeted by his magnificent hound whose coat, teeth, and face were covered with blood. The Prince cried out and panicked about the safety of his infant son. The man ran to the cradle which was empty.

The Prince, believing that Gelert had killed his son, drew his sword and plunged it to the hilt in his Wolfhound's chest. The dog let out a terrible death cry, which was met by the cry of the Prince's son, covered with blankets and untouched.

Next to the child was a slaughtered gigantic wolf, the source of the blood and Llewelyn's agonized comprehension.

It is said that Llewelyn never smiled again.

Further tales of their loyalty and prowess grace pages of Celtic life. Survivors of the Celtic ancients' attack on Delphi are filled with accounts of the huge animals fighting side by side with them.

Imagine the sight from the enemy front line.

Initially all one can see is dust thrown up by marching humans and dogs. As the gap between you shortens, you can make out shoulder-to-shoulder two-hundred-pound shaggy brindle animals with their tails erect. Panic clouds your mind.

Within minutes, your senses are bombarded with the sight of dogs breaking into a gallop, covering seven feet with each stride. Three-inch fangs and rows of tearing teeth jut from slathering mouths, and the dogs run without faltering, ignoring your puny armor, straight at your exposed throat.

~

I put down my studies, impressed. No wonder these dogs

were the prize of royalty from generation to generation. Brave and colossal, with the power to enforce either their master's wish or their own at a moment's notice, they are an intimidating breed.

Chapter Seventeen

Dogs Training Trainers

Poised to fight crime for his handler's protection.

It is a scorching day in August when I drive from the university in Fort Collins, Colorado to a secluded spot in the foothills near Denver. I make the trip to learn from a police-dog trainer. I hear that he will be discussing appropriate defensive postures when dealing with dog attacks during police work. What I see stays with me to this day.

I enter the compound completely unnoticed. There are a handful of casually dressed men, presumably police officers, crouched against the fence. They are facing a medium height, meticulously clad man with what appears to be heavy rubber armor across his chest and arms, massive gloves, and thick protection along his thighs and lower legs. He wears a mask that appears to let light in, but it too is heavily armored.

Attached to his Batman-like gloves is a German Shepherd Dog, bloody foam fizzing out of his jaws and flecking the man's thighs. The animal alternately wrenches the man's arm, then butts at it to get a deeper grip. The man lifts the dog off her front feet with enormous effort by raising his arm. The dog relinquishes her grip and begins grabbing at his encased thighs, bowing and then lunging repeatedly at the man.

He eventually raises his hand when he has his fill, and the animal is collected and tethered by the trainer.

I know that this battle of man against dog is staged for a learning exercise. This awareness did not stamp out my imagining how horrific the contest would have been without the armor.

Yet I am gripped to watch further.

After several other policemen are subjected to an onslaught by other German Shepherd Dogs, the trainer brought out a Pit Bull.

"This breed," he says in a slow methodical way, emphasizing the contest we are about to see, "has three times the compression power of the German Shepherd Dog. This is due to the enlarged temporalis muscle which connects to his jaw.

"They also have an innate drive to hang on. Sometimes you can break up their bite by placing a stick behind the premolars and forcing the jaw open.

"There is a lot of mystique behind these dogs. They are usually docile unless provoked." He twirled the baton to let the games begin.

The police officer gave a loud "Oof" when the meaty, compact dog impacted his chest. He staggered backward, lost his balance, and fell. The dog attacked the man's flailing arm before the handler could reach him. He gripped the man's wrist and shook his bullet-shaped head while the man shrieked.

The handler repeatedly commanded the dog to stop, yet time seemed to grind to a halt while the wrenching was carried out in slow motion. The handler rushed to the officer, kneeling and reaching out his hand. The policeman recovered his balance, ignored the advances of the handler, and walked toward his comrades mumbling about how he could feel the dog's teeth even through the protection.

I needed to see this demonstration. My only experience with dog attacks had been when I was three. I had a personal encounter between a Pekinese and my upper lip while attempting to pet her. I remember running and crying to my mother with blood streaming out of my lip and pouring onto the front of my blouse, my bloody hands reaching for her trousers. Otherwise, all I had till that moment was book learning.

Though I had often seen the effects of "Big Dog vs. Little Dog" in the Emergency Room at the Hospital Teaching Clinic, I had precious little understanding of the ripping and shearing forces of an incited dog. Or of their repeated onslaught.

Driving back to the Teaching Hospital, I marveled that most of the time, these animals kept their vicious side veiled from humans. Of course, they produced the occasional bark or growl related to the postman or laundry flapping menacingly on the clothesline, but for the most part, they were truly domesticated.

But that wild dog is always there.

CHAPTER EIGHTEEN

DOG LONG-SUFFERING

When it is yours, it's always different.

Where I go to work, my daughter Anastasia goes to work. We have a family business where animals just happen to be part of the family.

I wish to teach her how to treat family. You take care of their health issues as soon as they crop up.

Shortly after clearing the dishes one evening, when we are sitting companionably on the couch, I reach over to Luke, our mixed-breed rescue dog. Lifting the heavily-pigmented lip over his upper canine tooth, I say, "Luke needs his teeth cleaned." Without thinking, I chip a little tartar off the crown of the tooth at the gum's edge. This is a carryover from the old days, when vets didn't have beautiful digital X-ray machines to see what was happening below the gum line. We just cracked the tartar off.

Anastasia holds him off food the next day, and we load Luke into the car like every other trip to the vet. The eerie thing is, I have no premonition as to the grief we are about to experience.

Hooked up to the gas anesthesia, Luke looks like any other giant dog. And I look like any other doctor getting a little spray in the face from the dental machine. Midway through the procedure, Anastasia takes a break from her studying, sidling up alongside me to point out a wart-like lesion on the upper gum. As I replace my glasses with magnification lenses, I see what looks like a cauliflower floret, rigidly sessile.

I examine Luke's entire mouth and the lymph nodes draining it. There are no other similar outcroppings.

"It's nothing," I tell my daughter. "It's probably a wart."

"If it were someone else's dog, wouldn't you recommend that they biopsy it?" she replies in her seven-year-old wisdom.

I pause in the cleaning process and look at her. "Yes, I guess I would." I replace the ultrasonic cleanser in its holder on the dental cleaning machine, next to the brand-new polisher and spritzer. I stare at the immaculate row of tools, feeling for the first time an ache and queasiness in my stomach.

"Nothing but the best for our Luke," I say lightly, as though it is all the same to me. As though I can fool my own daughter.

I remove a dollop of the growth, and place it in the histopathology jar for the pathologist to read the result. That doctor is miles separated in distance and objectivity.

There is no bleeding from the section I cut out, so I decide to harvest a larger sample, in fact the whole mass.

It is more invasive than I first realize. There is bony involvement on the end closest to his nose. I remove everything that I can, using a curette to scrape the bone clean. This time, there is blood.

I quickly make a sliding graft of gum and suture the flap of tissue over the defect: stitch, stitch, stitch. Absorbable suture so that I do not need to go back and remove it at a later date from the tender gum.

The courier comes at midday to pick up Luke's sample

along with several others. By this time, I am engaged in other business. Other clients demand my attention.

I thrust the situation to the back of my mind until the nasty results are faxed from Dr. Potter's laboratory. Luke has an adenocarcinoma. It's an aggressive cancer. The paper and its diagnosis sit before me in black and white. The stark fact is that he has very few months to live.

I wish I could say I went home to hug Luke or telephone my daughter at school, or did some other productive thing that day. What I did is to bury myself in work, at least until I got home. First thing I see after parking the car in the garage is Luke, wagging his tail, sitting on the gold-colored leather sofa as though his world had not cracked apart.

I examine his oral wound, hoping that it holds the secret of his later treatment. No roadmap there.

To whom do I tell the news? It's a family problem now.

I cannot break down; must be the strong one. Holding my voice steady, I deliver the news over the phone to my husband who is working a late shift. We decide that until we have come to agreement about a solution, we will not break the news to Anastasia. She and I eat dinner in our regular kitchen with regular plates, but nothing else feels quite real. But I pat Luke and hug him and talk about school.

The next day, the technicians position Luke on the radiology table. First one side of his chest is subjected to the radiation; then the other. In the final position he is laid on his back in a blue foam padded trough. The *Rrrr* of the machine thuds into my chest cavity; that's how hollow I feel. I know he must be confused, with his paws upended above his head, the fine feathers on the backs of his wrists suddenly looking shaggy and worn.

The radiographs are negative for any spread of the cancer. Cancer? Is that really what is wrong? Can we get that second opinion?

Calling local veterinary oncologists confirms my suspicions; it is very unlikely that a pathologist would sign a paper saying that an animal had cancer and not be greater than ninety-nine percent certain of his diagnosis. He probably even sought a second opinion himself.

For the specialists to help me further, I will need to bring Luke in for a skilled exam and explore the possibilities of radiation.

Irradiating him five days a week. Under sedation.

This treatment may provide no more than a six-month extension of Luke's lifespan.

I thank the oncologist, for after all, she is doing her job for me and countless others. But then the sobbing begins. I begin the depression part of the grief cycle. Back and forth I will vacillate between the stages of bargaining and anger, depression and denial. Eventually, I will come to accept the inevitable. But there are many other stones in the wall first.

My husband and I recognize Luke's unique character and spirit. He is not a "people person." He would be scared out of his mind to be carted back and forth to a hospital five mornings a week, placed on a table, tranquilized, have an endotracheal tube placed down his throat, and have his mouth irradiated. Then awake to hazy sights and sounds of other caged animals. Disorientation daily.

Besides which, we are informed, tissue in the mouth will likely slough, dead, from inside and outside of his mouth. He may be disfigured and painful.

He does not appear painful yet, and we tell ourselves that

the best of our intuition about his level of comfort and conscious state dictates that the lesser of two evils involves keeping him at home and trying a medical substitute for radiation.
We will be able to decide on a day-to-day basis if he seems
too painful, or there is a decline in his spirit.

The other option is final. We are not ready to accept finality,
not without a significant deterioration in his joy of life.

The decision that we agree to make, that we decide is in
his best interest, may or not have been the correct one.

I tell my daughter about Luke's cancer on the night after
her eighth birthday. That is the occasion on which she decides
to ask if we had received the notice back from the pathologist.

I hesitate. "Yes, it is cancer," I reply, apparently in too low
a voice to hear.

"What?" she asks. "I can't make out what you are saying."

"The pathologist says it is cancer," I repeat. "It's cancer, and
an aggressive kind. It can spread anywhere in the body. But
usually to the lungs."

"How do we know it's spreading? How are we going to
treat him?"

"We have a drug to treat him with. We decided against
radiation because it would be too difficult with the kind of
personality that he has," I reply.

Though this was twenty-five years ago, I still remember
the empathy and alignment I felt with Luke. The spirit that
expressed itself a certain way, in Luke alone, made him the
precious dog he was.

Every procedure we do for him will test that spirit till
the end.

Anastasia becomes the self-elected person to daily check
his mouth. His giant head rests on her lap. His body follows

the contour of the gold couch. When he is settled, she strokes his coat until he reaches a blissful state of ignorance about her mission. She proceeds to lift the slobbery lip. Her finger runs along the gum.

It is five months before the cauliflower returns. Innocent, light pink petals blister the gum. Nothing shouts malignancy.

"Mort," I say, standing playfully over his back and twisting his hair between my fingers, "I've got to get you into surgery."

Mort turns his head to me with an expression of undying love and trust. What is that kinship that I feel, looking into his expansive pupils; something as close as any human being's attention?

I don't want to disappoint him. He does nothing to disappoint me.

Scheduling even my own dog on short notice is difficult. The tumor has tripled in size. I imagine he feels its roughness every time his tongue grooms his mouth.

As the anesthetic takes hold, I avoid those pupils.

I feel...distant. I hear nothing, not the rhythmic breathing. Nor the heart monitor.

The neoplasm has no desire to peel out with a simple blade. It rigidly adheres to the skull like a barnacle on a ship's hull. Because of the angle of the monster, the only radiographs I can take are poor quality and I abandon that project.

With the emotion of a robot, I drill the bone surrounding the growth. It feels like a sponge. There is no calcium latticework holding it together.

I revert to dental tools. The work stretches out to infinity. I take a brief bathroom break and forge onward.

He will need his pain medication replenished before waking up.

Again, I fashion a living bandage of gum tissue. Again, I send every scrap of tissue to the pathologist.

Luke awakes slowly. His head is in Anastasia's lap. Blood drools on her purple skirt. He manages a weak salute—a wag of his tail.

"Be quiet," she says tenderly. "You've got cancer."

By the weekend, Luke has recovered from the worst of his oral pain. He's over the wooziness. He can lift his leg. On the fourth day post-op when he attends to this business, I notice unmistakable crimson fluid coming from his bladder.

Blood in his urine. On the list of side effects of his chemotherapy, this is extremely rare. Like anyone who cannot believe the evidence of their senses, I examine and re-examine his urine. It's blood, more blood than urine.

It's not the cancer causing the blood. It's caused by what is supposed to cure him.

A fancy white envelope brings the anticipated news. It's as though the pathologist wanted to shroud the painful experience of opening the inevitable. 'Neoplastic cells grow up to the edges' of the sample.

Mort can no longer control where he urinates. We come home to small and large puddles of urine on the couches, the floor, and the carpets.

Whoever wrote guidelines on euthanasia vs. hospice care was my best friend. Does your dog have more good days than bad? Does he still enjoy his activities? Is he losing weight? Can you accommodate his changes in behavior? Does he have his five senses about him?

But those questions weren't enough. I added my essentials. Is he making a spiritual connection with us? Does he regret making a mess in the house? Does he keep his head on his forepaws, listening to an unseen drummer? Would a person in a similar situation experience unbearable pain? Does he show pleasure or connection with daily experiences?

Am I keeping him alive just because I can't bear the torture of losing him?

There was no discrete answer. It was a continuum of pain. Luke's situation wrenched the answer out of our hearts: keep him alive. Clear everything out of the basement except for his bedding; stop the chemotherapy; start twice daily pain medication.

My plight is not lost on my staff members. I stammer when I discuss euthanasia with clients. I blubber in the bathroom between appointments. I thank everyone for their patience with me, and yet when I go home to Luke, he is loving and active. He plays with the other dogs. Apparently spiritually well.

My family holds up better than me. I hear my husband's snoring. My sleep is frequently interrupted by agonizing over our boy's treatments.

My daughter plays in the usual way with her big man. She asks few questions.

I pray for a sign. I feel like I am fraying at the ends.

One day, when I get home later than usual, I see that Luke has not soiled the basement. Nothing on the plastic sheets. Nothing in his bedding or on the walls. I follow him outside and watch him strain. No urine comes out. He is quiet about it, but in whatever position he holds his trigger leg, either up in the air or on all fours, he has no success.

"I'm taking him into the clinic," I tell my husband. No one offers to go along, and I do not want assistance.

Luke awkwardly arranges his spine so that he can get into the car. His bulk seems exaggerated to me that night.

The twenty minutes to the clinic seem chilly. I slide down in my seat to help me resist the temptation to speed. Luke licks the back of my hair.

"Yes, I will help you my son."

At the big barn-red door, I hesitate. Finding the correct key, I have the premonition that this will be the last time Luke accompanies me through these doors. I begin to sob.

Through the buckets of saline flowing out of my eyes, I turn on the lights to first the lobby, and then the treatment room. Lazily, almost tentatively, Luke follows, his fully furred body nearly obliterating the doorway's opening.

Controlling my spasming larynx, I walk to the lovely purple medium nitrile gloves. I place sterile lubricant liberally over the index finger.

"This is not a decision made by me alone," I say out loud, swallowing hard. "I have to consult with my family."

Within a centimeter of the anal opening, my finger outlines a smooth capsule belonging to a mass that shouldn't be there. For an instant, I imagine it in my mind's eye—grey blobby fingers, not arranged in an organized fashion like normal colon tissue.

And for the first time, Luke cries.

Not for the pain, I tell myself. But because he is leaving us behind and he will miss us. I can't even imagine how much we will miss him.

I telephone my husband.

"He is ready to go. He has a tumor in his rectum that feels like the size of lemon."

There is no answer.

"Do you want to come down?"

I can envision his head forcing the phone back and forth in a 'no.'

"Talk to Anastasia and call me back?" I ask.

There is a pause then, while the phone is fumbled and dropped.

"Anastasia? Can you talk to me about Luke?"

She is very reserved. "Put him to sleep," she says, with a voice uncommon for her. "Put him to sleep right now."

"I'll see you at home." I ring off.

I realize Luke is still vocalizing, making a sound somewhere between a cry and a growl, that clearly my family members must have heard. He is straining to urinate on the tile.

I speak to him in a respectful manner while I unlock the controlled substances box.

I withdraw the ochre-colored fluid from its container, forcing my diaphragm to inspire as I go. And still, many years later, I can feel this as complete connectedness with my companion.

Waiting for his spasms to dissipate, I request that he lays down, and he obeys. I extend his right front leg toward me and shave a small patch on it. He licks it once, marking the spot for me. I take the alcohol bottle in my right hand and splash a little on his vein.

Then I butt my head up against his, so that we are connected, arm and head. I repeat, "You are a good boy. You are such a good boy," and hold off his cephalic vein with my left hand.

It springs up.

I have a moment of anxiety that I cannot complete this on my own.

I tell him, "I am going to put you out of pain so that you

will never have to go through this agony again. Duncan and Anastasia and I will miss you." By then, I have completed the injection, and the familiar head is slumping against me, eagerly being called to rest.

I cover him with a sheet.

The familiar sound of Duncan's car draws me out of the building. The moon is full and creamy in appearance, and I yearn to howl at it to voice my grief.

Duncan stops at the sheet and we embrace, uncertain what to do next and leaning on each other for support. We eventually break the clinch, and both of us assist Luke to the holding area, where we keep pets until the crematorium can pick them up.

I don't think that I want more of his fur than already crowds the house, but I cut a lock and place some medical tape on the small clump. I take his collar and tags.

All of this I have walked people through scores of times, and yet the meaning penetrates in a new way.

I want a shrine to this dog, to never forget his spirit. His unselfish heart that gives depth to that saying, "I wish I could be the person my dog believes I am."

CHAPTER NINETEEN

DOG WITH FOREIGN BODY

What goes in does not necessarily come out.

foreign:

6 a: occurring in an abnormal situation in the living body and often introduced from outside; i.e. a foreign body lodged in the esophagus.

body:

3a :a mass of matter distinct from other masses.

b :something that embodies or gives concrete reality to a thing

~Merriam Webster

For your average dog, it is not always enough to have an object on the outside of the body. It may not be sufficient to paw a favorite toy until all the stuffing comes out of it. It is inadequate to nuzzle it, throw it in the air, cuddle it, torment the cat with it, or leave it, covered with slobber, behind the couch cushions.

No, you need to swallow it whole. The richness of the object can only be appreciated gastronomically, when it is lodged safely and for days in the outflow tract of the stomach or in the small intestine. And what a variety of objects I have personally removed from there. Handballs, strings off a basted turkey, bones, thongs, pantyhose, needles, fishhooks, popsicle sticks, a "mute" button from a TV remote, stuffed mice intended for cats, scarves, gym socks, dish towels, stuffed toys intended for children, a crochet hook, objects d'art, and so on. Once, I retrieved a skewer from a corn dog that was sticking all the way out of the stomach through the skin. The dog's owner had dubbed the dog "Pupsicle." Another client told me how she had bought her son a Christmas present which produced warm, flexible toys from a special batter, and her son had fed over forty of them to the dog. They needed to be surgically removed.

Because these objects lodge in certain parts of the anatomy which are not easy to access, surgery is often necessary to remove them. The patient, innocent of all that must be done, sleeps peacefully through a procedure that is usually thrillingly successful. Many dogs do not even seem to miss a day before they are ready to become repeat offenders. Because no matter how careful we are to keep them from finding the perfect object to swallow, they lie in wait for the perfect moment; the sleek soft stuffed animal that is dropped by the toddler, or the fishing line that still smells of fresh bait.

It may seem that the veterinarian should easily be able to determine what has happened with her patient. This is an example of a particularly difficult situation.

Mrs. Toos waits expectantly in the exam room with Fluffy, a Maltese female.

"She won't raise her head," says the owner.

"Let's put her on the table so that I can examine her," I reply.

Fluffy is hoisted on the table by the technician, where she looks around expectantly. I cradle her head and move it in all directions gently and slowly. She does not resist.

I move to her front legs. She lets me move them through range of motion exercises without so much as a peep.

Meanwhile, Ms. Toos is showing me videos of Fluffy playing with the cat. They are both very flexible, and the little Maltese rolls on her back and runs circles around the cat.

I place Fluffy on the floor, letting her find her own way around the room. She does not limp, she stretches her neck out, she trots and walks equally well, and then she sits up against the exam room wall, pushing her rear end against the barrier, and placing her legs last. An unusual way to sit down.

"She was absolutely fine until the last twenty-four hours," the client asserts. The technician picks her up again and places her on the examining surface. I palpate her spine for pain, lumps or bumps, and then stretch her rear legs out as far as I can, to ascertain that they are even. Nothing is crooked. There is no cracking such as I feel when there is arthritis. I cannot convince myself that this is a traumatic incident, but the client keeps mentioning symptoms like trauma.

"What shall we do, doctor?" she says.

I look at her and her pet, who is eleven years old. I am concerned that Fluffy may have an internal problem, such as diabetes or pancreatitis, that is the true source of her pain. "I think we should run blood tests. We may need X-rays also, but let's see first what the lab work is showing us." She agrees to the tests after viewing an estimate, and I leave the room. Immediately the door opens, and she rushes out after me.

"Doctor, come quickly, she's doing it again. She never acts like this."

I hurry back to the room, and see the little white dog lying with her head on her front feet, perfectly still.

"OK, Mrs. Toos," I reassure her. "We will figure it out. The technician will get her blood tests. Let's get her an anti-inflammatory in the meantime."

We have a long discussion about her easily upset tummy and that she cannot eat corn or wheat so that most pills are out of the question. We agree on an injectable medication as the best way to help her for this episode, and the owner takes her patient home after the blood tests and urine are captured.

About five o'clock that evening, I call her home and talk to her husband. He has a lot of questions about her condition, and assures me that the patient is at home, trembling and shaking.

"Why won't she lift her head?"

We discussed that Fluffy can hold her head up, and did in the exam room, and that she seems to have no spinal spasms. I let him know that there are several good emergency clinics in the area, and that if he thinks there are issues with her neck, we are lucky to be supplied with some of the best radiologists and neurologists in the world. I urge him to take Fluffy there. After ten minutes discussing the pros and cons of going to a specialist, I ask him if there is anything else to throw light on her condition. He says, "Well it's probably out in left field, because she's a really well-trained dog when it comes to the trash. But, there was another dog over a couple of nights ago, and he's not that well-trained. I had a whole bunch of shrimp that I had been cleaning a couple of days before, and the other dog knocked over the trash can and spread the shrimp tails all over. My dog might have eaten one or two. Do you think this could have anything to do with it?"

Chapter Twenty

Dog Refusing To Obey

He takes great pleasure in being contrary.

M_{ax} is my rescued three-year-old Labrador Retriever. His history is that he has been passed around between four adult members of a family for over a year. One day, a cousin brings him into the clinic and smacks him on his head when he disobeys her.

"Nothing will get him to mind," she says, exasperated.

Max is taken away from her directly; papers are signed; he becomes a ward of the clinic. Promptly, he is assigned to an intake run where he has plenty of food, water, exercise, and cozy blankets.

Max does not appreciate the change in scenery. Snarling and growling, he plasters himself at the far end of the run and does not approach anything that his humans give him. The photo of him on the "Please adopt this dog in need" webpage shows a black, snarling beast with saliva dripping in long ropes from both sides of his mouth. Not adoptable.

On the fifth day of this debacle, one of the volunteers employs a trick she has perfected, which is to use peanut butter on the assumption that his drive for food will overcome his desire to bite someone.

This volunteer is a smallish woman. She has the skill to attract animals to her, especially those in trouble or damaged emotionally.

While I queue up behind her, she holds out a tentative edible prize—peanut butter on a cracker. More snarling ensues.

Then she places some on the side wall of the kennel, near the front door.

"Max," she calls softly, "Here Max."

She backs away, nearly running into the crowd that has gathered behind her.

"One at a time," she asks quietly. The throng disperses.

Someone hunts down a leash. Max makes a tentative eye movement in the direction of the peanut butter.

Two more morsels of peanut butter seem to calm the terror within him. The technician slowly opens the chain link door and throws the leash as a lasso over Max's head. He balks, then relents, gulping the peanut butter in sticky spoonfuls into his parched mouth.

No sensible person would assume after this beginning that they could take this animal home and have them clearly trained and mollified within a week's time. I clearly am no sensible person.

I sincerely believe that I can restore his damaged spirit.

At every lunch break, I take Max out into the play yard or on leash for a spin around the neighborhood. Thousands of animals have not taught me the lesson that my own pet could in a few minutes. Max is strong. Far and away too strong for me.

He pulls me all over the blacktop.

One of the staff members eventually sees our plight, and

brings us a harness that resembles a hackamore in a horse. It keeps his head down, but he still charges ahead with his neck bent. Then we try a strap that threads through the chest area and slows Max down, but does not stop the pulling entirely.

The brawn contained in those front legs, powered by the pectoral muscles, is astonishing.

Still I take him home, certain of my ability to teach obedience. Drawing on years, even decades of experience, I still am unable to appreciate at times the independent will of an animal and the physical and mental capacity they possess to bring their will into being.

I always believe my will is stronger. I must believe this when I am performing an unwanted exam on an animal, poking and injecting and thoroughly handling every cracked tooth and unwanted growth on their body. It is an agreement that most animals make grudgingly, some happily, and some make not at all. Those few unhappy canines and felines I seek assistance with, either using a strong person or a piece of leather surrounding the muzzle.

Some stare me down. Some menace and lunge, overpowering their owner's grip and grazing me with clenched lips. Those animals I am clever enough to avoid, respect, or examine from afar.

But I am not clever enough to avoid Max. Many times, I ask myself why I made such a beeline for him. Is it because he is such a handsome boy? Is it a control issue, where I see myself as the gentle lion tamer? He just made my heart turn over when I saw him. Not the first time this has happened; definitely not the last.

He's adorable. But not even slightly obedient. He just needs time, patience, and retraining, or so I console myself. He came from an abusive background, and he needs to re-learn that love is unconditional. His good behavior will be rewarded, and his bad behavior will be ignored.

This is what the trainers have told me, as they back out the door. More than one has refused to work with him, and has been at the opposite end of the leash when he lunged at them.

If I leave anything on any table anywhere, including a pen or my embroidered cap or even a spring-loaded brown sugar-filled container, he will grab it and make mincemeat of it. I can have the trash behind a cabinet door under the sink, and if he can wiggle his nose in, I come home to trash and decimated pieces of molded plastic everywhere.

The water dispenser which saves us from drinking sulfur-tasting well water is a particular favorite. Even though my husband velcro-ed a plastic shield over the front of the hot and cold water taps, he has found a way to slake his thirst in the sloppiest possible way, distributing morsels of fresh water all over the kitchen carpet.

No more wool carpets. Nothing on the counters. Child proof locks on the kitchen cabinets. Toilet seats down. Familiarity with short black hairs on all the couches.

Clearly, I need to stick to writing rather than enforcing obedience.

CHAPTER TWENTY-ONE

TRENCHMOUTH

How does she tolerate the situation? She gives new meaning to the word stoicism.

Chipper bounds into the exam room sporting a harness attached to a frilly dress with black and yellow polka dots. She has been extensively trained to run into a room, sit in adorable fashion, and breathe expectantly while waiting for the action to begin.

"She's such a well-behaved little dog," says her owner, a petite blonde with hair as well coiffed as her Pomeranian. "I hardly ever need to give her treats any more."

"She looks very sleek," I agree harmoniously. "I would love to take a look at her. What is she here for today?"

"In spite of everything we do, we cannot free her of her odor."

I remove the little patient from the floor, placing her rear feet on the table and cradling her front end in my arms. "Where do you think the odor is coming from?" I inquire.

"Well," she says, hiding her face with her hand as she speaks conspiratorially, "honestly it smells like her butt." She giggles timidly.

I suspend the little creature above me, to look things over from the bottom up.

There is no odor from this end. Tail and surrounding areas are normal.

I gently replace my forearm across her ribcage. Tilting her head, I am subjected to an odor like rotting food. I know this odor well.

She is suffering from deteriorating bone and gums from infection.

In short, rotten teeth.

Lifting her compliant upper lip, I view the hair wrapped around her gums, one-quarter inch layer of solid pus, and exposed tooth roots indicating severe, constant pain and periodontal disease.

The disease takes its name from the periodontal ligament, whose unpraised job in life is to hold the tooth fast to the bone of the jaw, and be flexible enough to cushion the grinding and tearing motion of the teeth. Using the suffix '-itis' indicates inflammation or disease, leading to the word and condition of periodontitis.

I muse that although a large proportion of dogs over three are purported to have periodontal disease, very few have the condition to this extreme. Those that are so affected, where every chew they take is laden with pain and mobile teeth, make an impression on me.

Considering the exaggerated degree of pain she is suffering, she hides it well beneath her bouncy exterior and fancy outfits. Her struggle to avoid attention from her owner can only be defined as stoic. She would no more lash out at the woman because of chronic pain than the sun would stop in its daily arc.

Dogs have been presented to me with all manner of painful conditions from fractured femurs to eyes popped out of their heads; still sporting a loving tail wag even while covered with blood. Enduring this condition which can be easily solved encourages me to present my solution wholeheartedly.

"Ms. Sims, you may never have endured tooth pain, especially not to the degree that little Chipper has, but let me show you the pus that has built up on her teeth."

I scrape a portion off with a tweezer and lay it on a sponge pledget.

"Several million bacteria are making a home in her mouth.

"In addition, there are strands of Pomeranian hair wound around her teeth at the gum line and they bite into the painful bone that has been exposed." I pull several of the colored hairs out of the diseased mouth, Chipper cooperating in the friendliest of manners.

Then I point to crumbling teeth. "Chipper is so young, that I hate to have to remove teeth, but if we don't I'm afraid she will sicken from heart valve illness, or even chronic urinary problems from these bacteria."

"Oh yes, doctor, I forgot to tell you that she is marking all over the house now. I got so hung up on the smell…"

She lowered her eyes. "We don't have to put her to sleep, do we? I would die if that happens." She dug in her purse for her wallet, showing me a picture of how she appeared at the same time last year.

"I feel so responsible. They told me about this last year, and I barely listened. I assumed they were just finding a way to make more money."

Her eyes were glistening.

I said, "There is a good chance that after a few days of slightly uncomfortable recovery, she will feel even more chipper, if that is possible. We have the best pain medications available to ease her through the next few days."

She signed the surgery consent form and escorted Chipper to her temporary condo.

Festering wounds are always painful, be they in the mouth, the skin, or deep in the muscle, as in a cat bite abscess. The offending teeth were removed surgically, and Chipper recovered uneventfully, to live many years free of pain.

Part Three
WIRED-UP

Scientists (and others!) are fascinated about the functioning of the dog brain. The anatomy of human brains is strikingly similar to dogs, which implies a certain correspondence with our mental processes.

What do dogs observe? Are all their responses instinctual or do they have the ability to reason? Thanks to sophisticated equipment, we can measure certain mental tasks. We find that they are likely to employ the same parts of the brain as we do.

CHAPTER TWENTY-TWO

DOGS IN AN MRI

That which distinguishes man from lower animals is not the understanding of articulate sounds, for as everyone knows, dogs understand many words and sentences. In this respect, they are at the same age of development as infants between ages of ten months and two years that cannot yet utter a single word.

The Descent of Man and *Selection in Relation to Sex*
~Charles Darwin

The technician makes last minute adjustments to his MRI device. He has been waiting expectantly for this day.

For weeks, he trains eleven dogs to first approach and then lie still in the scanner. The dogs chosen represent a variety of temperaments. There are several pure breeds; the rest mutts. Garden variety pets.

He repeatedly flips the on-off switch to accustom his clients to the loud vibrating clicks and clanking made by the machine.

Final preparation consists of getting them accustomed to having their heads held rigidly by a plastic device. This keeps the dog motionless in the guts of the machine during a very unnatural experience. Not only is the machine loud, but it is confining, and the dog's field of vision is very restricted.

The researcher worries that these dogs might feel claustrophobic.

"We use lots of praise, lots of positive reinforcement," he says.

All the dogs pass the final tests with flying colors. They even pose for an amusing group picture lounging against the MRI after the final run through.

The best eleven dogs and a control group of twenty-two human volunteers listen to a battery of over 200 sounds. The purpose is to have the MRI evaluate specific functions of their brains.

Do dogs process sounds in their environment the same way that we do?

The researcher starts with noises that he believes will not have an emotional impact on the animals such as a train whistling and a car door closing. Eventually, he tests sounds that may cause feelings of tenseness in the animals such as bouts of crying and hysterical laughter. He also plays the racket of angry barking and the heart-tugging sounds of whimpering.

Not surprisingly, all participants, human and canine alike respond most strongly to emotionally charged sounds. The section of their brain which "lights up" in the MRI scanner is very special and extremely specific to the primary hearing area of the brain. Anatomically, it is called the anterior part of the temporal lobe.

In other words, the receiver in the canine brain is in the same place as in our brain. With connections running to all areas of the canine brain and body from this area, it is sophisticated, and differentiates significant sounds from background noise.

It is in exactly the same area of the human brain where sounds are captured and processed.

"We do know there are 'voice areas' in human brains, areas

that respond more strongly to human sounds than any other types of sounds," Dr. Andics, spokesman for the research project, explains.

"The location (of the activity) in the dog brain is very similar to where we found it in the human brain. The fact that these areas exist at all in the dog brain is a surprise. It is the first time we have seen this in a non-primate."

The experimenters concluded, "We think dogs and humans have a very similar mechanism to process emotional information."

Just a few years after the previous study, on Aug. 4, 2015, HealthDay News reports a landmark study by Gregory Berns, a neuroscientist, and his colleagues at Emory University in Atlanta, Georgia. Senior author Berns details his conclusions after studying canines' ability to recognize human faces.

Because dogs are such highly social animals, he explains, they need ways to recognize those important to them.

He states in the article, "Our findings show that dogs have an innate way to process faces in their brains, a quality that has previously only been well-documented in humans and other primates."

The discovery of this face-processing section in the same neurologically rich area of the temporal cortex which recognizes emotional sounds may help explain why dogs are so sensitive to human social cues.

"Dogs are obviously highly social animals, so it makes sense that they would respond to faces. We wanted to know whether that response is learned or innate," says Berns, who leads the Dog Project in the university's psychology department.

The six dogs in this study are successfully trained to enter a similar MRI machine similarly to the Hungarian project and remain motionless during scanning. Dr. Berns is able to train them without the need for head restraints or sedation. Their brains are scanned while alternatively being shown videos of faces and everyday objects.

The MRI shows heavy activity in the dogs' temporal lobe; however, the response is greatest when they see human and dog faces. Everyday objects show little response.

The researchers name this region the "dog face area." The findings appear to indicate that dogs are born with an innate response to faces.

If it was a learned response—for example, if they associated a human face with food—then faces would trigger a response in the reward region of their brains, Berns asserts.

When it comes to people, there are at least three face-processing regions in the brain. Being able to identify faces is important for any social animal, the researchers suggest.

"Dogs have been co-habitating with humans longer than any other animal," author Daniel Dilks, an assistant professor of psychology at Emory, says in the news release.

"Understanding more about canine cognition and perception may tell us more about social interaction and perception in general," he concludes.

It certainly tells us more about dogs.

Chapter Twenty-Three

Dog As The Reasoning Animal

Man is the Reasoning Animal. Such is the claim. I think it is open to dispute. Indeed, my experiments have proven to me that he is the Unreasoning Animal... In truth, man is incurably foolish. Simple things which other animals easily learn, he is incapable of learning. Among my experiments was this. In an hour I taught a cat and a dog to be friends. I put them in a cage. In another hour I taught them to be friends with a rabbit. In the course of two days I was able to add a fox, a goose, a squirrel and some doves. Finally, a monkey. They lived together in peace; even affectionately.

Next, in another cage I confined an Irish Catholic from Tipperary, and as soon as he seemed tame I added a Scotch Presbyterian from Aberdeen. Next a Turk from Constantinople; a Greek Christian from Crete; an Armenian; a Methodist from the wilds of Arkansas; a Buddhist from China; a Brahman from Benares. Finally, a Salvation Army Colonel from Wapping. Then I stayed away for two whole days. When I came back to note results, the cage of Higher Animals was all right, but in the other, there was but a chaos of gory odds and ends of turbans and fezzes and plaids and bones and flesh-not a specimen left alive. These Reasoning Animals had disagreed on a theological detail and carried the matter to a Higher Court.

Letters from the Earth: Uncensored Writings
~Mark Twain,

It is a significant fact that the more the habits of any particular animal are studied by a naturalist, the more he attributes to reason and the less to unlearned instincts.

The Descent of Man and Selection in Relation to Sex
~Charles Darwin

I am riveted to my chair. It is late evening in my second year of veterinary school. There, on the "Idiot Box," two dogs are facing each other, one crouched in an apparent invitation to play.

The voice-over questions whether these two dogs, or any dogs for that matter, can act except by instinct. It states that dogs have no conscious awareness of their actions. No one, the voice asserts, can "prove" that the dogs know they are playing.

Meanwhile, the camera rolls, showing these dogs raising up on their rear legs, pretending to bite one another. Eventually the Malamute rolls on his back and from there invites play, a highly evolved form of interaction.

This idea of instinct-only canines is like taking a snapshot of a dog and insisting it is the same as a full-blooded animal.

Can dogs reason, or do they act purely on instinct?

Of course, instinct rules when they feel terror. Their sphincters relax, their pupils widen, and hormones of fight or flight flood their bodies. When food is placed in front of them, instinct demands that they eat it (depending on how picky they are). When a female dog is in heat, they breed. But not all dogs act in the same way to the same stimulus. Their wiring is much more complex than this.

The theory of instinct says that all dogs will respond the same no matter what stimulus is presented to them. By this theory, every Chihuahua should eat whatever is presented to him. There is no allowance in this concept for the tiny dog that refuses everything except hand-fed chicken. It is clear that food alone is not always a motivator. Maybe instead of just instinct, dogs have common sense. Who wouldn't want hand-delivered food rather than dry pellets?

To explore this subject further, we need to know more about the brain of that animal that sleeps on your bed. When we know more about how she or he is made, surely that will help solve the puzzle.

Incredibly, humans and dogs both have nearly identical "primitive" brains. These sturdy, perfectly-formed organs wake us up in the morning, regulate our breathing and ensure a heartbeat. They relay intricate messages to every other part of the body so that it will function according to the rhythm of the heart and breath.

If we could peer into the womb at thirty days of development, it would be very difficult to tell the difference between a human embryo and a dog embryo. What we might see is the convoluted brain at the rear of our skull, called the cerebellum, developing in a very similar manner in both humans and dogs. It coordinates movement and position in space. Picture the awkward movements of a very young puppy or child as she attempts to walk without swaying, and you will appreciate the cerebellum's role.

At this point, only thirty days into development, one hundred-sixty million cells in the white and grey matter of the cerebral cortex have already hooked up, manufacturing neurotransmitters to signal each other. Little brain lobes are forming. One will be the center for auditory or hearing signals. One will cover olfaction, or smell. Another large area will be the visual switching station for the developing puppy or human.

Can dogs reason? Brain cells gather information from everywhere on the animal's body, blasting signals from the one side of the brain to the other at speeds of 119 meters per second. Every time this happens, he uses a special band of nerve tissue. This group of brain fibers, called the corpus callosum, is also present in every human being allowing them to integrate complex information and make decisions.

For example, how does an animal know how to react when it perceives pain? He or she knows because higher mammals' nervous systems, full of essential information, stretch from the brain to the farthest reach of the body. Tiny sensory organs—identical to human beings—sense touch and pain and heat. Dogs can feel, and they have the sense to move away from whatever is obnoxious. But here, I believe, instinct ends and reason begins.

When a certain dog is in pain, he will hunch up and cry. Another painful dog will inform his master by barking for excessive attention. A third will bear the pain stoically. Dog's ability to recall old injuries and act on what got attention (positive or negative) in the past seems akin to ours. Does that constitute the ability to reason? It seems clear that all three dogs decide how to react based on past occurrences. They even appear to make a different determination based on current circumstances. For example, today the mistress is home with the kids, so the dog gets extra food by blatantly begging and whining. When the master is at home, the dog may be more successful by lying at his feet.

In fact, some people believe dogs are capable of abstract thought. When a dog begs to play with a tennis ball stored in the garage where he cannot see it, it seems clear that he has a mental picture of an object that is not in his field of vision. When he moves from the couch to the front door at five o'clock in the afternoon, he appears to have a mental picture of the owner that will soon materialize. When he waits outside the bedroom door until you let the cat out to play, he must have conscious awareness that there is a living creature in there that he can have fun with.

By anyone's definition, wouldn't this be labelled reason?

Part Four
HEROICS

Everyday heroic acts by dogs are so commonplace that they might be taken for granted. Note the Yorkie that sits in quiet friendship with the lonely older person, the Collie who warns his owner that the man's blood sugar is reaching frighteningly high levels, or the Beagle who bites down on the cell phone to dial 911 when his owner has a seizure. As part of their job, some dogs detect land mines or bombs, sniff for cancer cells, or act as companion animals to soldiers suffering from PTSD.

Because these acts are such a part of a dog's nature, I dedicate an entire series to this aspect of their character.

CHAPTER TWENTY-FOUR

DOG AS FIRST RESPONDER

There are no schools for dogs demonstrating life-saving techniques; no classes any dog would ever take that demonstrate the Heimlich maneuver. Yet repeatedly, we find that these beings are tuned in to the point of unimagined acts of kindness to us humans.

Toby is a Golden Retriever belonging to Debbie Parkhust. Toby lives with another dog in the Parkhurst home. Toby owes his life to the Parkhursts. He was originally rescued from a dumpster by Debbie and her husband.

Debbie Parkhurst is a 45-year-old jewelry artist living in Calvert, Maryland. Debbie was working on a piece of jewelry when she decided to take a break and slice an apple for a snack. She was home alone. One of the pieces became lodged in her windpipe. It completely cut off her ability to breathe. After throwing herself against a chair to attempt to dislodge it, she started beating her fists against her chest. She believes this alerted Toby to the problem.

"The next thing I know, Toby's up on his hind feet and he's got his front paws on my shoulders," she reported to the local newspaper, the *Cecil Whig*. "He pushed me to the ground, and once I was on my back, he began jumping up and down on my chest."

Toby's jumping apparently managed to dislodge the apple from Parkhurst's windpipe.

"As soon as I started breathing, he stopped and began licking my face, as if to keep me from passing out," she said.

"I, literally, have pawprint-shaped bruises on my chest," Parkhurst said. "I'm still a little hoarse, but otherwise, I'm OK."

A friend took Parkhurst to the doctor.

"The doctor said I probably wouldn't be here without Toby," Parkhurst said. "I keep looking at him and saying, 'You're amazing."

At first, Parkhurst thought Toby was simply trying to play.

Now she believes the Golden Retriever knew exactly what he was doing.

"I know it sounds a little weird, but I think he had a sense of what was happening," Parkhurst said Monday. "Of all the dogs in the world, I never would have expected this goofy one here to know the Heimlich."

As strange as Parkhurst's story might sound, Toby's actions actually followed the emergency measures recommended for choking victims by the American Heart Association and the American Red Cross.

Both agencies recommend first aid responders use a series of five back blows followed by a series of five abdominal thrusts, otherwise known as the "five and five."

"I have no idea where he learned it from," Parkhurst said. "But I can tell you that I'm going to peel and mash my apples from now on."

CHAPTER TWENTY-FIVE

DOG WITH SNAKE

This dog stepped fearlessly into an act of courage while his owner his.

As Gerry Goodrich tells the story to me, he went to elaborate preparations to gather the appropriate gear needed for several nights in the Everglades. Gerry is an experienced camper, used to long hikes with seventy-pound packs into the Colorado wilderness. Gary makes extensive lists, then pares them down to the essentials he will need for himself, his precious four-year-old daughter, and his dog Jack.

Conscientiously, he loads the big family tent, a smaller pup tent, sleeping bags, human and dog food, and cooking gear into the trunk of the family car. On the seat of the rear part of the car, he places his first aid gear, sunblock, sheathed knife, case of water, and toiletries.

Content with his purchases and packing, he buckles in his child, puts Jack into the rear seat, and leaves the family homestead to travel five hours to the Everglades. The trip is longer than he expects, and the windshield time makes him sleepy. He sets up camp in the dark, with Jack watching over the toddler and barking his approval after all have full stomachs and are ready to go to bed.

The next morning Gerry, his head still reluctantly spinning

with thoughts of work, yawns and wakes up slowly to his surroundings. As he rouses himself, his mind languorously switches to the necessities: replenishing the fire that burned low last night, and making coffee from some left over grounds of the day before. Then he will start some flapjacks for his daughter. He has even, he remembered, brought real maple syrup.

Gerry is not thinking of the intuitive power of dogs at this moment. He is not even considering his dog, Jack, the one-eyed cattle dog that has been a member of the family for six years. But he stumbles over the animal when he gets out of the tent and takes a step toward the picnic table where his supplies are.

He stumbles over the dog, because there is Jack, rigid as a sawhorse, staring under the table.

The man almost ignores the animal's growl, because he so rarely hears it. Then Jack begins barking as though his larynx will burst.

Gerry, unused to this behavior, feels completely out of his element. He begins repeatedly chattering at him, "What's going on? What's wrong with you?" Later, he recalls experiencing a cold wave rush through him.

He bends over to look under the table. This is where the dog's attention is directed.

There, mouth wide open, is a Water Moccasin snake, one of the deadliest reptiles in the United States. Its jaws are agape so that the man can see the cottonmouth throat, for which the snake is nicknamed. It has a thick, sausage-like dark brown body, with a tiny tail. Gerry says that it may have been his imagination, but it looked like the leaves were rustling around him as his tail rattled.

The snake was laid out in an S-shape. Gerry caught himself trying to calculate the distance this animal could strike.

"I knew instantly that the snake could not reach me or my daughter with its venom, but I nevertheless hid behind my dog! I found myself unable to think clearly, unable to make an offensive move during this showdown, and eventually the snake slid away out of my sight.

"My dog was clearly much more of a hero than me in this instance. But what I cannot figure out is how did he know it was his responsibility to save us from the snake, instead of saving his own hide? How did he know that this was a pit viper, a venomous snake, when he plays with black racers in the backyard all the time and has never so far as I know been exposed to a venomous snake?

"Instinct? Or true caring for my daughter and me?"

CHAPTER TWENTY-SIX

DOG IN COMBAT

Four pounds of treasure won in a poker game.

Bill Wynne crouched on the deck of his transport ship during combat. The anti-aircraft fire was intense, and his boat's deck was booming and rocking under him. There was so much smoke and fire pouring out of the deck that he was half-dazed, and unable to determine which way to turn. Eight men next to him had already been leveled.

Eight men.

Confused, Bill looked around him, hoping against hope that his Yorkshire terrier could have survived the assault. He had purchased her when he was in New Guinea for six dollars and forty-four cents (two Australian pounds) from a comrade who was losing a poker game and needed the money.

Bill was completely attached to his four-pound friend. She had been with him through miles of slogging around in a backpack, and had survived 150 air raids with him when he was stationed in New Guinea. This is where he had first been united with her. One of the other soldiers had found her in a foxhole and couldn't tell if she belonged to the Japanese or to the Allies. They had even taken her to a prisoner of war camp to see if she knew Japanese commands. No one had been able to break the secret of how a tiny dog had been found in a foxhole.

Bill knew his situation was dire. His mind reeled to the time Smoky had survived a typhoon at Okinawa. She had eaten from his rations, and lived without veterinary care in the jungle, running on coral beds that sliced up other dogs' pads. She had flown 12 air/sea reconnaissance missions without a complaint. She had even drifted down to earth on a parachute specially made for her by Bill and his buddies who loved her. She had been his ever-present companion in the South Pacific.

Wynne turned his attention to the hazard he was in. Suddenly, out of the smoke the little terrier appeared, running away from the direction where he knelt. The man followed the toy dog, who stopped and waited repeatedly as she drew her master out of certain death. Though the boat was badly damaged, Wynne and Smoky were saved.

Wynne called Smoky, "My angel from a foxhole."

Certain that Smoky had more to show the whole world, and that her talents should not be hoarded, Wynne began with his comrades' help to teach her tricks to entertain the troops. A natural at show business, Smoky learned complicated tricks quickly and even learned how to maneuver blindfolded on a tightrope.

After her two year stint in the war, she became a huge hit, starring in her own TV show. She also entertained at hospitals, and later met and comforted hundreds of hospitalized soldiers. She was lauded as being the first therapy dog.

At the age of fourteen, she was laid to rest with beautiful eulogies from Bill and others who had known about the special touch she gave to everyone who knew her. with a lovely trophy atop her grave.

Smoky was one of those special creatures that could live one life to the utmost and then, when that life was successfully concluded, she creatively lived a second one in service to others.

CHAPTER TWENTY-SEVEN

DOGS AS AVALANCHE RESCUE

Carrying on a thousand-year-old tradition.

The Alpine Mastiff jerked his head away from his task to respond to the monk's voice. "Here, here!" came the frantic call.

The dog was torn. He had located the faint odor of human under the soft snow where the man had slid off the road while pursuing his fallen horse during the avalanche. It was too late for the horse that had disappeared from the trail at twenty-five hundred treacherous meters above sea level. But Barry's focus had been on rescuing the man left behind, and his gigantic heft and weight were thrown into the task of digging through the avalanche slush, rapidly forming a great pile of snow behind him as he excavated the man.

"Barry! Barry!" his master sounded the outcry again. "Barry!"

With one final stroke, Barry broke through the snow covering the man's face, and heeded his master's call. When he reached his keeper, he saw the small, twisted body of a child. The monk was kneeling, weeping over the tiny body. Barry had never seen his master so distraught.

The monks who lived at the stone house on this Alpine divide had dedicated their lives to helping travelers across

146

this pass. Because the weather could change on a moment to moment basis, many of these travelers would be caught with insufficient covering for the blast of frigid air and temperatures that dropped regularly into the single digits.

Since Roman times, people had traversed this pass between Switzerland and Italy. Their intentions had not always been good. Robbers were sure to lie in wait for any merchant that braved the alpine divide, relieving him of his steed as surely as they removed his goods. In addition, penitents walked this way, making a pilgrimage and demonstrating their desire to seek forgiveness for their wrongdoings. Many of these were penniless.

They were joined by soldiers of fortune, mercenaries seeking riches by fighting for any country that would pay them. In addition, day laborers made the trek across the divide.

But it made no difference to the monks if a traveler was a tax collector or someone running from the law. Beginning in the eleventh century, all were welcome at the stone house for shelter, food, and lodging. Bernard of Menthon, later declared a saint, saw the need to protect and provide those who made the treacherous journey. The hospice that bears his name has been run by Augustinian monks for nearly 1000 years.

For the past several hundred of those years, a collaboration between man and beast has sprung to life. Local guides working for the monks originally took dogs on their patrol, beginning in the mid-seventeenth century. Originally, the dogs sense of smell and direction was counted on to locate and recover snow-covered paths. These animals were massive Alpine dogs with short coats that would not take on extra weight from ice and snow. Their claws allowed them to clutch the snow better than any ice cleats, and their flexible pads insured a safe grip. Often, the guide would work with two at a time, so that one dog could be sent back to alert the monastery, and the other could unearth a trapped individual or reach a person overcome by exhaustion.

It is estimated that over two thousand lives have been saved by these methods. Early photographs show a group of men placidly eating around the large table at the stone house, with outsize dogs weaving in and out of the travelers.

One special dog, born in 1800, is particularly of note. Though archivists kept no individual records on any animal, there was one dog named Barry who is reputed to have saved over forty lives. He was particularly keen on working the trails with both his masters and other dogs. Remarkably, he and other Saint's Dogs that lived at the monastery raised the next generation of puppies in such a way that the immature adults learned how to break trails, save travelers, and cooperate with another dog in doing the saint's work.

There are stories that still circulate that Barry saved a young boy trapped in an ice cave and brought him back to his father and mother. The boy was said to have gripped his coat and been carried back, half-dead, to his family. Other stories say that the mother did not survive the avalanche. Again, since there are no individual archives, nothing of this rescue can be collaborated. Regardless, the heroics of this dog and all those that bested the weather day in and day out to look for lost and buried travelers is undisputed. Barry was so admired for the number of lives that he saved—estimated between forty and one hundred—that up until the very recent present there was always a dog at the hospice named after him.

Barry died at the ripe old age of fourteen in Bern, Switzerland. There are no archives to show how Barry made this journey or how he lived two years after his move from the monastery, yet St. Bernard's wishes were continued by the monks and their dogs for over a hundred fifty years since his death. We do know that during heavy avalanche seasons, many dogs lost their lives, and the monks made the decision to carry on the breed by introducing the size and vitality of the Newfoundland dog.

Though the Alpine/St. Bernard dogs were large—some nearly two hundred pounds—the Newfies were larger, and they had a much heavier coat. They did not have the dense tight fur that the Alpine breeds had developed to keep heat in and repel snow and ice. This led to unforeseen hazards, as the full weight of the ice and snow gripping their fur kept them from being light-footed. Some of these animals weighed nearly three hundred pounds, and they could not manage the same exploits as the Alpine Mastiffs.

In 2005, a new chapter unfolded in the thousand-year-old history of the St. Bernard dogs. It was decided that the Barry Foundation would take over the care and the breeding of the dogs.

Because the dogs had been called into service for hundreds of years, some of the offspring were used as therapy dogs in hospitals where people were lonely and needed the gift of touch. This was very different work for the St. Bernards. Not all could perform this service, as it meant lots of petting and physical touch from a variety of people. However, all that were capable of this assistance went into it faithfully.

As for the mountain pass, helicopter missions now replace the brave avalanche dogs.

CHAPTER TWENTY-EIGHT

DOGS GRIEVING

His heart belonged to Jon, the Navy hero.

Jon Tumilson was a competitor from the time he was in grade school. He was heavily involved in body-contact sports, including wrestling and martial arts.

Family members recall that Jon wanted to enlist in the special forces from the time he was very young. He kept his body fit and his mind sharp to deal with the demands he would encounter, first in his training, then in his chosen profession as a Navy SEAL.

Jon also had a soft spot for dogs, especially Labrador Retrievers, and his family opened their home to Hawkeye, a black dog with the typical amazing ability to follow his nose, hunt, and be a close companion to his master.

Tragically, when Jon Tumilson was 35 he was one of 30 American troops, including 22 Navy SEALs, who were killed. A Taliban insurgent shot down his Chinook helicopter with a rocket-propelled grenade on Aug. 6, 2011.

His body was returned from Afghanistan to Rockford Iowa, which was his hometown. Shortly thereafter, a funeral service was held for the hero.

Tumilson lay in a coffin, draped in an American flag, in front of a tearful audience mourning his death.

Tumilson's Labrador Retriever, Hawkeye, became part of the ceremony. Hawkeye was such a huge part of Tumilson's life that Jon's family let the dog precede them down the aisle.

They entered the service in front of a capacity crowd in the gymnasium at the Rudd-Rockford-Marble Rock Community School. Hawkeye then followed Tumilson's good friend, Scott Nichols, as Nichols approached the stage to give a speech. As Nichols began his speech memorializing his friend, Hawkeye walked up to the casket and then dropped down with a heaving sigh in front of his master's casket as 1500 mourners witnessed him accompanying his master until the end. He gave mute tribute during the entire service.

A relative, Mr. Pembleton, lauded Mr. Tomlinson while Hawkeye kept watch. About Jon, he remarked, "To say that he was an amazing man doesn't do him justice. The loss of Jon to his family, military family and friends is immeasurable."

After the ceremony, Mr. Nichols and his kin welcomed Hawkeye into their family of dogs and people.

PART FIVE

EARLY RELIGIONS

Great men and women have great ideas about the treatment and care of animals. Many religions teach us how to show regard for those living beings that share the earth with us. Others give us intimate details of the relationships between gods and their dogs.

Chapter Twenty-Nine

Dogs and Animism

Pythagoras has theories about the proper treatment of dogs as well as geometric equations.

The year is approximately 550 BC. A man wends his way through a Grecian open-air marketplace, ignoring the foodstuffs, the colorful fabrics, and the shopkeepers assailing him to purchase their wares. He has only one objective in mind, and it does not have to do with his comfort.

He stops in front of the animals for sale, tightly packed in makeshift cages or tethered in groups around a stake. The animals are intended for slaughter.

"What do you want for the whole lot of them?" the man asks.

The merchant looks at the man, mentally sizing up his clothing and expression. Why would anyone want this ill-assorted group of animals? Yet he can make a whole day's profit in one transaction. He quickly names a figure.

The two men agree on a price in the merchant's favor. The money is pocketed, and animals are removed in twos and threes from the bustling market.

The purchaser, named Pythagoras, wants only to set the animals free, and he removes them to the countryside where all are let go.

Pythagoras is an animist. He allows no spiritual separation between men and animals. In his opinion one spirit pervades the universe. His conviction is that both humans and non-humans possess souls.

This man who was an ardent animal rights activist, father of geometric theorems and a brilliant scientist lived in Greece approximately 580 to 500 BCE. Most people recognize his name because they were required to memorize and prove his mathematical theorems, but his views on spirituality and vegetarianism thrust him into the forefront of thinkers of any age.

Spirit, he believed, was indestructible; made of fire and air. Because of this, this energy known as the soul had to be delivered to another body at death. This occurred during reincarnation. Pythagoras' belief was that the life force was re-birthed from human to animal or animal to human, in a process called transmigration of the soul.

His views of the spirit did not stop there. One of the tenets of animism holds that various forces in nature, such as thunder, have souls. Even though he was a devoted scientist, he was not afraid to have his passion rule him and his discoveries.

He did not stop tinkering with his views of the spirit, including the treatment of animals. He refused to eat meat as part of his religion. He wrote little about dogs specifically, though he made mention of the fact that they are intelligent even though they do not have the power to express themselves through speech. That did not exclude the fact that animals can reason, sense, and feel just as humans do.

His views were echoed later in Judaism, which followed him by several hundred years. The guiding principle in Judaism is Tza'ar ba'alei chayim, a command to relieve suffering for all living beings. Many verses in the Bible and Talmud also cover the proper treatment of animals put into service. The tenderness and sensitivity showed by Pythagoras is echoed in another early religion called Zoroastrianism.

CHAPTER THIRTY

DOGS IN ZOROASTRIANISM

The following chapter uses a dog's voice to show the character, skill, and proper treatment of the dog. It describes an ancient monotheistic religion, predating Judaism and Christianity. This religion integrates dogs into everyday life and finds them to be essential in death.

A dog has the characters of eight sorts of people:

'He has the character of a priest,

'He has the character of a warrior,

'He has the character of a husbandman,

'He has the character of a strolling singer,

'He has the character of a thief,

'He has the character of a disu (beast),

'He has the character of a courtezan,

'He has the character of a child.

~The Avesta of the Zoroastrian Religion

I am Darius. Not Darius the First, the great emperor who ruled and expanded Persia, but a dog living freely and comfortably in the land he rules. I was born into a special era. I do not know much of politics or religion, only that a great prophet named Spitama Zarathushtra established a faith called Zoroastrianism.

Darius the First was fond of this prophet, and I too am fond of him because he went to great lengths to describe the beauty and even amusement of being a dog. Not only that, he included as part of his sacred texts guidelines for how humans are to treat us. He gave us canines previously unimagined freedom and respect.

Just listen as Zarathushtra's god, Azura Mazda (Wise One), talks about me. 'I, Ahura Mazda, have made (the dog) self-clothed and self-shod; watchful and wakeful; and sharp-toothed; born to take his food from man and to watch over man's goods. I, Ahura Mazda, have made the dog strong of body against the evil-doer, sound of mind and watchful over your goods.' What dog could want more than this?

He brings tears to my eyes when he recognizes my value in the household. 'And whosoever shall awake at his (my) voice, O Spitama Zarathushtra! neither shall the thief nor the wolf carry anything from his house, without his being warned; the wolf shall be smitten and torn to pieces; he is driven away, he melts away like snow.' Tears of joy flow down my cheeks when I read this.

But enough about me. I must tell you about Zarathushtra. He led a charmed life in ways, in that he lived till the ripe old age of seventy-seven. And at his death he had thousands upon thousands of adherents to his religion. However, some would consider him unlucky. He was thrown out of his homeland as a young man, and his life was brought to an end when he was assassinated by another prophet for his beliefs.

Though Zarathushtra gives new meaning to the phrase that a prophet is not appreciated in his own country, it is really difficult to determine what in his seemingly inoffensive teachings made him so hated. What did he do to others except emphasize their moral responsibility? What were his sins other than preaching the importance of a clear understanding of good and evil, so that a person could definitely support one side or the other? Being a dog, I do not see complications, especially those that would lead one to murder some ancient man.

Oh, I forgot to mention that he also taught it is the duty of a person to make friends out of one's own enemies, to make the wicked righteous, and to make the ignorant learned. At last, with persistence he caught the eye of a Persian ruler named Vishtaspa, who took him under his wing. Zarathushtra set to work compiling his beliefs and teachings into a sacred text called the Avesta.

Being a dog, I know how to play, and I think Zarathushtra was in his heart a very playful dog. Just read his poem about us creatures.

> 45. 'He eats the refuse, like a priest;
> he is easily satisfied, like a priest;
> he is patient, like a priest;
> he wants only a small piece of bread, like a priest;
> in these things he is like unto a priest.
> 'He marches in front, like a warrior;
> he fights for the beneficent cow, like a warrior;
> he goes first out of the house, like a warrior;
> in these things he is like unto a warrior.
> 46. 'He is watchful and sleeps lightly, like a husbandman;
> he goes first out of the house, like a husbandman;
> he returns last into the house, like a husbandman;
> in these things he is like unto a husbandman.
> 'He is fond of singing, like a strolling singer;
> he wounds him who gets too near, like a strolling singer;
> he is ill-trained, like a strolling singer;

he is changeful, like a strolling singer;
in these things he is like unto a strolling singer
47. 'He is fond of darkness, like a thief;
he prowls about in darkness, like a thief;
he is a shameless eater, like a thief;
he is therefore an unfaithful keeper, like a thief;
in these things he is like unto a thief.
'He is fond of darkness, like a disu;
he prowls about in darkness, like a disu;
he is a shameless eater, like a disu;
he is therefore an unfaithful keeper, like a disu;
in these things he is like unto a disu.
48. 'He is fond of singing, like a courtezan;
he wounds him who gets too near, like a courtezan;
he roams along the roads, like a courtezan;
he is ill-trained, like a courtezan;
he is changeful, like a courtezan;
in these things he is like unto a courtezan.
'He is fond of sleep, like a child;
he is tender like snow, like a child;
he is full of tongue, like a child;
he digs the earth with his paws, like a child;
in these things he is like unto a child.

If this description of my character were not entertaining enough, Zoroaster quickly grabs my attention with how I am to be fed. Of course, I would love milk and meat with lots of fat attached. And that is exactly what Zarathushtra recommends. Woe be to the person who would dare feed me spoiled meat, as severe penalties result including a series of whippings depending on whether I was an indoor dog or a hunting dog.

Incredibly even to me, injuring or killing one of my friends or relatives brings penalties as severe as harming or killing a man. Zarathushtra wrote this caution about what can be expected for a person who harms any of us, "Whosoever shall smite either a shepherd's dog, or a house-dog, or a Vohunazga (stray) dog, or a trained dog, his soul when passing to the other world, shall fly howling louder and more sorely grieved than the sheep does in the lofty forest where the wolf ranges."

Verse after verse describes the preciousness of my relatives when they are pregnant, likening them to a pregnant woman. I told you that I believe Zarathushtra had an inner dog, and you will agree with me after you see these requirements. If a sister-dog is found on or near your property, whether in your stable or field, fence or barn, it is your responsibility to take care of her. And even after her pups are whelped, it is man's responsibility to care for them for at least six months until they can subsist on their own and defend themselves. If you ignore these requirements, the punishment is stiff. 'If he shall not support her, so that the whelps come to grief, ...he shall pay for it the penalty for willful murder.' Come to think of it, I am becoming enlightened as to why other humans did not appreciate Zoroaster fully.

Let's move onward to treatment at death. Though I do not know Anubis personally, I know his body of work, and that he was a special dog who employed special workers. So, I am not surprised that when humans die, Zoroaster employs our special species in a trusted capacity. He clearly knows about our keen senses and the services that only dogs can provide. He searches among us for a special male dog greater than four months of age. This animal must be white with tawny ears, or with eyebrow fur that makes him look like he has four eyes. The dog performs the ritual of Sagdid, literally "dog sight" upon the person's body. During this procedure, the animal is called upon to scan the body with all his senses to determine if the person has any signs of life. If the Sagdid ritual declares him to be dead, he is really dead.

I never was called to be that four-month-old special dog. I have a coat of brown fur, and no tawny ears, or whatever is required. As I said, I am a house dog, with enough privileges for a lifetime. But I do admit to being jealous at times of all the attention that those dogs got. And these selected canine roles continue after the Sagdid ritual, triumphant evil powers surround the human body that cause it to putrefy. I understand that these powers are highly contaminating and particularly noxious to the earth where the body lies. I am clear that the earth suffers at the point of contact, and must be purified. I must confess to you that I wish for one day I had those tawny ears or four eyes so that I could purify the route over which the body was taken to be given back to the elements.

I would have liked one chance to drive away the corpse demon, Nasu. I wanted to be the one, just once, to drive away the Demon Nasu far to the regions of the north. I did listen raptly when my brother who had the privilege at five months of age told me that the demon scurried away in the shape of a raging fly, with knees and tail sticking out, droning without end, just like the foulest of the foul Khrafstras who is an evil agent from a different cycle of creation. But that is another story.

Now that the person is truly dead, and the body has been moved and purified, his or her soul must make the crossing of the Cinwad Puhl, or "bridge of the accumulator," appropriately named after the one who accumulates souls. The bridge lies on the peak of the cosmic, imaginary mountain Harbruz, with one end in the south terminating in paradise, and the other in the north where the journey begins.

Beneath the bridge is hell.

The crossing of the soul of the departed takes place three days after death, at the dawn of the fourth day. Of course, the soul must pass between two special dogs that guard the bridge. Again, I never served this function, being a house dog, but the ones who did guard the gate during my lifetime were very chatty about who crossed the bridge and who fell into hell. They stated to me that though every soul was accompanied by a number of gods, it was also tormented by an equal number of demons.

An intimidating god named Rasn weighs the good and the evil deeds of the soul on his spiritual balance. If the deceased is righteous, the soul is seen as a beautiful maiden. She personifies his deeds in life and together with the other gods crosses the bridge. If the soul is wicked, his den, or embodiment of spiritual attributes, appears as an ugly maiden. His spirit fails to cross the bridge and falls into hell. Thus, is the fate of human beings.

When the righteous soul wishes to cross the bridge, it becomes an avenue nine lances (ninety feet) wide. For the wicked it becomes narrow like a razor blade. For the righteous soul the crossing is very pleasant. When the wicked soul, on the other hand, steps onto the bridge, he falls into hell because of his coarseness and sharpness. His crossing is very unpleasant, as the smell of decaying bodies reaches him.

Everyday, we are of great value to humans, both in joy and in sorrow. Yet in the 1800s, sad to say, a reform movement gained momentum attacking all rites in which dogs are involved. In the current century, practices involving dogs have been wholly abandoned by the reformists. They must have had a huge influence on orthodox Zoroastrians also, because their practices have also been severely curtailed.

If I were able to call out to Zoroaster and be heard, my joy would know no bounds!

CHAPTER THIRTY-ONE

DOGS IN INDIA

In which I wear a marigold necklace as a badge of honor to my species.

Today, I am a celebrant. During the other 364 days of the year, I am a nuisance, even a human health hazard because I may carry rabies.

But today, during the moon's first blush, I wander through streets heavy with the smell of lighted incense. My forehead boasts the tika, a blaze of color placed by human fingers laden with red ochre powder mixed with yogurt. The one who marked me with this holy vermillion dot used a single swift stroke leading away from my eyes.

Today, I am fed offerings of milk, eggs, meat and even sel-roti. This is a ring-shaped treat similar to a donut. I eat all of them with gusto. I graciously accept the floral necklace made from marigolds that is a mark of respect and dignity. I hear humans talking about this malla, which symbolizes the prayers that they bestow on me and the other dogs milling about.

Every night during this five day festival, all the outdoor lights on people's houses are illuminated. The indoor lights are also set ablaze, and flowers appear everywhere in homes. It is a time to honor dogs in all their roles—as guard dogs, companions, and friends.

My great immortal ancestors, Shyana and Sabala, who guard the gateway to the hereafter, are worthy of this praise. The Festival of Lights recognizes the belief that the dog is a messenger of Yama, Lord of Death.

So, you will know more about the importance of this Lord, I will tell you about Yama. Yama is an important figure in the Rigveda, as the first mortal who died and found his way to the celestial dwelling places. He was a mortal and now is a Lord, or god. But this does not mean that he dwells in a pleasant place. He presides over Naraka, which is Hell or Purgatory, and makes his abode there. Some say he is the guardian of the cycle of life, or samsara, because he directs the soul appropriately.

After the departed person makes his or her way past my kin (the dogs guarding the gates) they are presented to Yama. He sends the souls to the appropriate Hell, or may return the soul to earth or Heaven. This may seem confusing, but because good and bad deeds are not considered to cancel each other out, the same soul may spend time in both Purgatory and Heaven.

Though I am not afraid of any man, I would like to have met Yama earlier, when he was represented as the cheerful king of departed ancestors. Now, he rides a terrifying buffalo and adorns his body with skulls threaded on necklaces and belts. When I see his likeness of a green or blue body with red eyes popping out of his sockets and intensely colored garments, I know why they say that he wields the leash to seize the lives of people about to die. This leash is securely held in one of his four hands, and a mace is held in another. This all increases his ability to strike fear in the hearts of those who have an impressive number of bad deeds.

But enough about Yama, who is celebrated more often than we dogs. Today, it is our day to remember that no other beast was considered responsible or worthy enough to guard the doors of Heaven, and wander the world as messengers of Yama. We cleave to and carry out the wishes of our master. Our role is to walk among men and women to protect their homes and lives.

Kukur-Tihar (Nepali for Dog's Day) is the day for humans to celebrate the dog. In order to please the dogs, they are going to meet at Heaven's doors after death, and to ensure they are allowed into Heaven, people maintain the 14th day of the lunar cycle in November just for this exalted purpose. The other days we mill around in excess numbers, not attached to any human.

This is the way of the world.

CHAPTER THIRTY-TWO

DOGS IN ANCIENT TRADITION

A Hindu epic of inestimable value begins and ends with stories about dogs. These tales demonstrate the depth of the spiritual relationship between people and dogs at the time of the writing of the poem.

Where can you find heroic deeds and betrayal, petty jealousies and improbable births, all in the context of warring tribes? This is only a tiny fraction of the excitement to be found in the Hindu text, the Mahabharata. This sacred text is three times longer than the Bible, narrating deeds and adventures of gods and battling families from India's rich history. It reworks and refashions familiar characters—including dogs—to achieve new roles.

This is the epic which opens with the theft of the cows/light that we visited in Samara's story. Lord Indra looks to the divine dog to help him recover his cattle.

There is a far greater tale than this.

Deva-shuni is not only the celestial dog, but the mother of all dogs in creation. She undertakes a perilous journey to sniff out the tracks of thieves. She is able to recover the cattle not just by her sense of smell, but by a more significant life lesson referred to as "the path of truth." Significantly, she regains much more than cattle. Through unselfish actions when she refuses to be bribed by the robbers, she recovers nourishment for mankind in the form of milk from the cows.

Indra heaps praise on her.

As his goddess in the guise of a dog, she is responsible not only as a divine retriever and follower of the path of truth, but also to roam the mortal world. As she does so, she witnesses people starving. Because she is a goddess, she creates water with which to irrigate their fields.

Samara's heart is also with her canine children, and she prevails upon Lord Indra to always supply them with sustenance and a worthwhile calling in life. As a result, two of her unique offspring become the right-hand dogs of the god Yama, Lord of Death.

Unique because they have observed their mother roam the earth in the service of humanity, and they will now roam the earth in the service of Yama, identifying people who are close to death. Also unique because of their appearance, with tawny-colored tufts of hair above their eyes giving them the appearance of four eyes.

According to the Rig Veda, there is only one way for a soul to travel in its journey to the afterworld. Instructions require the decedent to pass by a path guarded by two four-eyed dogs, or chaturaksh, the progeny of Sarama. Thus, dogs act, as in many cultures, to judge and accompany the passage of dead human beings. One of the essential roles of the Death Dog is to precede the decedent because there are many snares and pitfalls short of a final resting place. In this religion as in many others, it appears that the dead have passed out of their life only to be judged in the afterlife as to the quality of their character and deeds. If they are found wanting, it will be torturous to find rest.

The path to death is followed by everyone, yet how a person lives their life is idiosyncratic. The Mahabharata shows a moral order of the universe, a code of living if you will, that is referred to as Dharma. In order to avoid lengthy regret in the afterlife, these fundamental principles weigh heavily. They are demonstrated repeatedly in the body of the sacred text, while we wait till the end of the chronicle for a dog to resurface.

After lengthy wars and many adventures, King Yudhishtira and the four other Pandava brothers have retreated to the Himalayas to prepare for going to Heaven. They are followed by a dog. The dog appears to be unnamed, but he is essential to the story.

As the party ascends the Himalayas, all of them except for Yudhishtira and his dog faint and die. One by one they are left behind. The two survivors continue their journey.

Suddenly Indra appears in a gleaming chariot. Indra wants to take Yudhishtira, the most pious among the Pandava brothers, to heaven. During all the adventures they endured, he is the one who never strayed from the path of Dharma.

The king refuses to enter the chariot without his brothers and wife. Indra reassures him that they will soon be reunited as the others have already reached heaven.

Relieved, Yudhishtira then motions to his dog to enter the chariot with him so they can both enter heaven. But Indra has other ideas. He replies that because it is necessary to sit on the floor to eat, and no dogs can be allowed under those circumstances. Even more importantly, he claims that the dog's presence will defile heaven because the mere glance of a dog can remove the consecration of the sacraments.

Quietly but firmly, the king states that for him to abandon

his friend during his life's journey would be the utmost betrayal. The dog has been devoted to him during the loss of his brothers and wife. Yudhishtira cannot be happy in heaven for he would be lost without his brave and loyal companion. His morality is based on right living, and he will not sacrifice it for the chariot ride with the god.

Indra leaves him no choice but to stay with his dog. When the king makes his final decision, the animal unveils himself as the god Yamadharma. In the complex manner in which some Hindu literature is written, this god Yama, the god of Death, is also Yudhishtira's father. What was to all appearances a mere dog is in actuality a father who followed his son to heaven. Now in human form, the father praises his son, telling him that his compassion for all living beings is exemplary. The father is impressed that a dog has been as dear as his son's own brothers, and Yudhishtira's conduct will remain a shining example to all men for all times.

The king bows down to Yama and Indra. He enters the golden chariot victoriously. Soon, he reaches heaven where his brothers and wife are waiting. This is the end of the epic.

Chapter Thirty-Three

Finale

The dog by your side is a radical experiment in domestication, transformed through years of care and breeding into the magnificently-crafted creature you count on for companionship and protection. The complexity of their reactions often seems stunningly clever.

Dogs have been bred to be complementary to us. Their personalities enhance ours.

All this began with events lost so long ago that only myths remain of what transpired. Did an early god walk the earth with his dog, creating water and creatures as he moved along? Or did a prehistoric woman in a moment of genius use a scrap of meat to coax a snarling animal closer to the fire?

In whatever manner our thrilling early attempts at connecting with another species began, they started as a trickle, eventually became a stream, and finally unleashed a torrent as we responded to each other's needs. Discovering the things that we could do with our new-found friends seemed limitless, and continued to expand. Yet the basics are still there—companionship, loyalty, friendship, and nonjudgmental love.

When King Yudhishthira made his final ascent to heaven, he refused to enter the gates if his cherished dog could not accompany him. As I reflect on extensive experience with my clients, I propose that the majority of us relish the idea of inviting our dogs into a golden carriage and bringing them with us to our final destination.

About the Author

Fierce. Loyal. Brave. Keen Witted. Observant. Refuses to Shy Away from Danger. Does this sound like your Best Friend?

Dr. Jeannette Barnes has a passion for dogs that extends far beyond her calling as a veterinarian, and into the realm of history, anthropology and the shadowy regions of myth and lore—all inspired by their fascinating ancestry and development from wolves.

"All dogs, from the tiniest two-pound toy Yorkshire Terrier to the massive 200-pound Irish Wolfhound, emerged from this undomesticated animal," Dr. Barnes muses. "Do you want a small cuddly dog? Someone already developed the perfect dog just for you. How about a large, powerful hunting breed? Exactly the right dog exists. We've got dogs to sniff out cancer; dogs to dial 911; dogs as military heroes."

Inspired by the intimacy, longevity, and depth of the relationship between people and dogs, Dr. Barnes set out to show that dogs were not solely instinctive beings; but imbued with spirit and the desire for service.

"There is a spiritual connection between dogs and humans," she insists. "I believe they were designed to be man's helper. But more than that, they have a long and fascinating history with man, as hunters, companions, demi-gods, and as a source of beauty and pride.

I can think of no place I would rather be, than *In the Company of Dogs.*

Dr. Jeanette Barnes writes about the incredible variety of dogs in this world, and to their shared history with wolves, from her home in Florida.

Learn more at:

www.jeannettebarnesdvm.com

www.ingramcontent.com/pod-product-compliance
Lightning Source LLC
Chambersburg PA
CBHW060335030426
42336CB00011B/1361